EDUCATION TODAY: LANGUAGE TEACHING

Language Teaching in Action

To F. Gouin and H. E. Palmer,
two great students
of language teaching method

Language Teaching
in Action

LEO R. COLE

Modern Languages Adviser,
West Sussex

LONGMAN

LONGMAN GROUP LIMITED
London

*Associated companies, branches and representatives
throughout the world*

© Longman Group Ltd 1973

First published 1973
ISBN 0582 32094 1

Printed in Great Britain by
Western Printing Services Ltd,
Bristol

Contents

Preface

At least part of a teacher's training should be concerned with acquiring a sound knowledge of method and techniques. A critical attitude to established practice has to be fostered, of course, and we have to beware of dogma. However, faced with the daily challenge of the classroom, the teacher needs to make himself a skilled craftsman. This does not imply any narrowing of his general education, for when we begin to study in earnest matters of procedure and practice, it is not long before we find ourselves grappling with basic principles related to linguistics, educational psychology and the philosophy of education in general.

This book specifies ten fundamental conditions necessary for successful teaching and effective learning in the classroom situation. Each chapter deals not only with what the teacher should avoid but also with what he should do in terms of positive procedures. Our analysis of teacher and pupil performance in the classroom setting offers constructive suggestions to meet the ten conditions essential for good teaching practice.

One benefit resulting from the extension of foreign-language teaching across the ability range with both younger and older beginners is that it has urged upon us the necessity to think more about our objectives and to review, improve upon and expand our techniques. Foreign-language teaching does not always seem to fit too easily into the more flexible and progressive child-centred systems of learning now changing the face of many of our schools, but the linguist must accept the challenge and show that both a balance and a blending of traditional and newer patterns are possible. The contention underlying the techniques advocated in this book is that it is possible to meet the learner's needs within structural frameworks that assert the importance of the teacher's skills.

It is hoped that the book gives advice, help and guidance of a practical kind. To make it as useful as possible a selective bibliography has been provided. This covers basic texts on method, audio-visual aids, tape-recorders and language laboratories. There are also bibliographical notes for each chapter so that the reader can pursue his study and refer to materials which should be helpful in putting into practice the techniques advocated. The book has an empirical orientation and places the emphasis fairly and squarely on the more immediate realities of the classroom. It also recognises the audio-visual and oral-active approach which characterises the modern scene as the fundamental framework within which today's teachers must realise their full potential.

LEO R. COLE

I

Listening to the Children

Any framework of analysis used by the teacher when he wishes to examine critically his own lessons should contain as a central feature some reference to the balance between teacher-talk and pupil-talk. How much does the teacher say in a thirty- or forty-minute lesson compared with how much the learners say? Assessment of the ratio between the two can reveal, in some cases, a gross overweighting in favour of the teacher. The teacher talks for the greater proportion of the time, while the children sit in receptive mood and are offered few opportunities to respond orally.

We are not primarily concerned here with whether the teacher-talk is in English or in the foreign language. It is self-evident that children who never hear fluent French are not likely to learn how to understand the spoken language. We are talking about the tendency of the unwary teacher to dominate lessons with his own talk and not cultivate the oral powers of the learners. There is no denying that some children will always profit in some measure from hearing large amounts of spoken material in the foreign language. Such lessons can on occasion be extremely useful, in certain circumstances and with certain provisos which we develop below.

When a lesson is teacher-dominated the children usually sit fairly passively, in the physical sense at least, and quite heavy demands are made on them to concentrate and listen attentively to the teacher's voice. Some brighter children may well be able to give full concentration and listen carefully for long stretches, but it is often the case that the majority, after ten to fifteen minutes, become restless and frustrated. Unless the teacher has exceptional voice qualities and personality, most children find it difficult to hang on every fleeting utterance issuing from the teacher's lips.

Some children are not convinced of the importance of language, and it is easier for them to lapse into their private dream-world and let the patter flow half-heeded over their heads. If the teacher wishes to aid and abet them in sealing themselves off in this way there are three means of doing so: speak with a loud, booming voice; speak quickly and nervously, pronouncing some words softly and indistinctly; or speak in a rather mechanical fashion, draining the sentences of all meaning.

Let it not be thought that it is young and inexperienced teachers who are always the ones at fault on the score of dominating lessons with their own talk. I have often observed the most experienced of teachers doing the same thing. The children are called upon to say very little. Sometimes the teacher has an excellent command of the spoken language; his oral fluency is admirable, and we remain bewitched. Although we may well fall under the spell of such talented performers at first acquaintance, we soon realise, if we shift our attention to the children themselves, that there is something wrong with the lesson. And what is wrong is the sad lack of interchange, the lack of active participation of the learners, the failure to draw out and cultivate the hidden talents of the disciples.

It is often the case that with the kind of lesson we are here criticising, the teacher may have an exceptionally vigorous, lively and dominant personality. The children will humbly submit to such a teacher's superior talents, and this humble submission may be a necessary first step in making them willing and ready learners. But if, after securing the docility of his class, the teacher continues to regard the children as an appreciative audience, and if, after months and sometimes years, the children gape in wonder at the authority before them, there will never take place that progressive development of the learner's skill in handling the spoken language that we so urgently need.

There is a phase in the language-teaching process in which it is most important for the children to listen carefully to whole stretches of the language spoken at normal speed. This phase usually figures as the initial one in a sequence which involves a number of varying techniques, and it can be termed the 'presentation' or 'demonstration' phase. Failure to expose the children to a good deal of talk will be the subject of our seventh chapter. The early stages of a school programme will lay heavy emphasis on the development of aural comprehension, and this will require that the children hear a good deal of spoken French, not necessarily from a single source. The kind of lesson in which the teacher might be doing a good deal of talking in the foreign language while the children sit and listen can fulfil a useful function, therefore, if it comes at the right point in a properly prepared programme.

Not only is it necessary for teacher-talk to operate at the appropriate phase and stage of the teaching programme, but also it needs to be accompanied by a wealth of visual material, by suitable demonstration and by a variety of movement and gesture. These contingencies will provide words and sentences with context and meaning, and they will also help in maintaining the interest of the class.

There is yet another condition which is a prerequisite if children are to derive maximum benefit from teacher-talk in the foreign language. They have to be trained in techniques of observation and discrimination: they need to know exactly what they should be doing when listening. Teacher-talk can have a variety of purposes according to the nature of the exercise being undertaken. For example, there will be times when the teacher is presenting and demonstrating the meaning and use of new sentence patterns and new vocabulary items. At other times he will want the class to catch only the general sense, the gist, of what he is saying. On other occasions he will want the pupils to discriminate carefully between sentences which are the same apart from one or two single sounds, or the same apart from intonation and so on. At one end of the spectrum we have extensive work involving a kind of subconscious aural assimilation, while at the other extreme we have more specific intensive work involving conscious assimilation on the part of the learners.

We have so far pointed out a number of factors which can, if

3

implemented, make teacher-talk in the foreign language successful and effective rather than boring and useless: using such talk at appropriate phases of a programme; using it in conjunction with visual material; using appropriate facial expression, mime and gesture; training pupils to observe different purposes in different kinds of talk. All too often these essential concomitants are neglected and their neglect usually leads to failure. A further feature related to these points and concerned with the talk itself now needs stressing: pitching the talk at the children's level of comprehension and achieving progressively more as the children move from year to year.

The good teacher will be aware of what each of his pupils knows in terms of vocabulary and mastery of structures and grammar points. He will know what ground in the syllabus he has covered, where more practice is needed and who needs the practice. This enables him to keep a high degree of control over the linguistic content of his talk in the foreign language, and to adjust the level to the varying needs of different classes. These classes will differ in ability and in attainment: each succeeding year of study should require a higher level of talk from the teacher in terms of vocabulary, structures and even speed, fluency and complexity of sentence utterances. In most cases the teacher needs to use, in the first instance, only those vocabulary items and sentence patterns known thoroughly by his class. There should come a point, however, where a small number of new words will gradually 'seep into' his talk, and such words will gather their meanings from context and situation. Some meanings may not become absolutely clear until after many repetitions of a word on different occasions in different sentence contexts. Generally, however, ninety per cent of the sentences uttered will be understood, and certain stock classroom expressions will recur many times in almost every lesson. The ultimate, though usually impossible, objective is to keep in circulation the segments of spoken language already acquired by the class.

Too many teachers who dominate lessons with their own talk fail to control the exact linguistic content of the sentences they utter and adjust rather haphazardly to the classes with which they come into contact. The Fourth Year pupils are approached with the same patter as the Second Year, some talk in a Third Year class may well be more complex in structure than the talk in a Fifth Year class, and so on: progression in degree of difficulty, in wealth of vocabulary, in length of statement, is impossible to detect.

Linked to the failure to control the level of the spoken language is the failure to check comprehension at regular intervals. The very fact that pupils are not allowed opportunities to respond in some way inevitably means there is no checking and no feedback. And it is certainly a naïve practice to ask the children whether they have understood what has been said. It is far better to check comprehension by seeing whether an individual pupil can give a correct oral response to a carefully framed question in the foreign language.

Before checking and testing whether individuals have understood the meaning of what has been said, there is a far more basic requirement which too often is not met. This requirement is that every individual in the class should be concentrating on what the teacher is saying, should be listening attentively. Children cannot do this unless they are trained to do so, and it is indeed the most difficult thing for the inexperienced teacher to achieve. Unless the children are giving their fullest attention and are intent upon the meaning of the sentences spoken by the teacher, so much talk is energy wasted. Only through the use of varied techniques and colourful, interesting visual materials, presented in a lively manner, can the teacher hope to engage and maintain the attention of the class. All forms of oral work demand for their success good personal relationships between the teacher and individual pupils.

The exact manner in which checks on comprehension are made should form part and parcel of good teaching method. Developing sound procedures in this matter should constitute a central aspect in the teacher's training. To be able to frame in precise terms the appropriate question to evoke a specific sentence pattern or word group is both an art and a craft that needs knowledge, skill, training and practice. What elements the individual pupil has or has not grasped can always be judged and defined by a close observation of his oral responses.

5

We have already noted that even some of the most experienced of teachers are at fault in dominating lessons with their own talk. Since this is so, it is worthwhile to ask why this should be the case: why does the experienced teacher do it? Where lies the real motive, the psychological justification for his doing this? Among the many reasons that are put forward there is a basic one not always readily admitted: that pupil participation on any grand scale slows down and disrupts the lesson. When lacking in confidence and under pressure, an individual child may speak inaudibly so that he has to be asked to repeat what he has said. A pupil may be too shy even to give any vocal response, or he will produce a faltering incorrect response. Some pupils may well seize the opportunity to make their companions laugh, and with ensuing chatter throughout the class it is difficult for the teacher to regain attention without raising his voice or reprimanding the class in some way. His solution is therefore to avoid creating such situations, and the easiest way to do this is to monopolise the lesson time. Such a solution, however, will never lead individual pupils to speak up with confidence, to develop their oral fluency and to enjoy taking part in the lesson. To achieve these objectives the teacher must look to improving his skill and technique as a craftsman in the classroom and to establishing a pleasant atmosphere and a relaxed, yet firm discipline.

It should be clear from what has been written so far that it is not teacher-talk in itself we are criticising, but rather an excess of it executed without regard to the conditions outlined in preceding paragraphs. What is bad is that a whole lesson of thirty to forty minutes is mainly characterised by teacher-talk and that this kind of lesson becomes the rule of the day. It is all too easy for this type of lesson to become a matter of routine: the teacher becomes set in his habit of operating in like manner every day of the week with whatever class he is taking.

If the teacher wishes to guard against the fault we are here examining, he needs first to recognise it by critically reviewing how he has operated during any given lesson. It is useful for him to ask himself at the end of a lesson such pertinent questions as the following:

How many opportunities were given for the class to say something together?

How much was said in the foreign language by how many individual children?

About how many children said nothing during the lesson?

The teacher may well consider these questions as particularly relevant to a certain age group or to a certain part of his total teaching programme, but if he is not satisfied with the answers, he should make sure that he develops his skill with question work so that the children are brought more into the picture. They need to respond to the material and participate in the activity of the lesson.

2

Using Audio-visual Aids

With the growing provision of all kinds of aids and equipment in the classroom it is important to exploit these instruments to the full and to harness them for the purpose of more effective learning. The contribution to be made by audio and visual aids, used either in a supplementary capacity or as an integral part of the main course, depends very much on the knowledge and skill of the teacher. The teacher needs not only to be competent in the practical operation of mechanical or electronic equipment but also to know the rôle and function of each specific aid in relation to teaching the foreign language.

In spite of the plethora of useful aids finding their way into schools, there are still teachers who make minimal or no use of aids at their disposal. Objects and pictures are sometimes entirely absent, and the lesson can proceed without a single reference to anything other than the printed text in a book and a few words written on the blackboard. Chalk, talk and text are the basic ingredients of the lesson and maximum demands are on the teacher himself. Although there exist imaginative teachers who are able to give interesting, lively and effective lessons without resorting to the use of visual aids, it is more often the case that the lesson without illustration lacks excitement, colour and life. Many children in the class will find restriction to talk, chalk and text not only boring but distasteful. The necessary repetition in language teaching can be tempered by interesting visual material, without which effective learning and retention is that much less likely to occur.

Visual aids can be divided into two basic classes: those that

8

require some form of equipment (projected visuals) and those that require no mechanical equipment (non-projected visuals). Of the first type are filmstrips and slides, transparencies for use on the overhead projector, cassette cineloops, 8mm and 16mm films and television or videotaped programmes. Of the second type there is a whole range of materials: real objects, models and toys, specially designed pictures, photographs, drawings and symbols, wallcharts, flannelgraph figurines, sets of cards, and so on. Audio aids include the record player, the tape-recorder and the language laboratory, apart from the sound-track on different kinds of film.

Not all language teachers are blessed with a perfect accent, intonation and pronunciation in the foreign language. And not all teachers may be as orally fluent as they would wish. The children in the class of such teachers (assuming these rely on their own resources) cannot expect to achieve great heights of perfection and fluency in the spoken language. Exposure to a pronunciation which is less than perfect, to oral delivery which is slow and never in more than small segments, to a limited amount of the spoken language, will sooner or later take its toll on the children. The growth of their powers of speech will be stunted. In such circumstances a wide use of native models on tape can be a great boon, provided of course that sound reproduction is first-class and issues from a good tape-recorder, preferably with extension speaker.

Even where the teacher is fairly fluent in the foreign language it is helpful for the children to hear other voices of varying pace on the tape-recorder. This is specially important once the pupil is past the early stages of language learning. These statements, questions, exclamations, dialogues, conversations and narrative passages issuing from the tape will be male and female voices; they will include the voices of children, of younger and older adults. Through being exposed to a range of authentic models the children will have opportunities to develop their powers of aural discrimination: their ears will become attuned to the natural rhythm, stresses, intonation patterns, liaisons and general pronunciation of the foreign language. These native models can be repeated as many times as may be considered necessary. With older pupils who have studied the language for a number of years the radio can play an important rôle in the development of aural comprehension.

In normal classroom circumstances the individual pupil often has extremely limited opportunities for giving an oral response. Choral work is often used sparingly after the first few years. In classes of thirty or more pupils it is only the language laboratory that demands that each child simultaneously should make a number of oral responses. Only with intensive speaking practice can individual pupils ever hope to gain any degree of oral proficiency. One rather ironic and disturbing situation which is not all that uncommon is when a rather dull teacher-dominated lesson actually takes place in an audio-active laboratory with the equipment lying for ever dormant. The same absurdity exists where tape-recorders remain unused on a side-table or hidden in a cupboard.

A lesson in which oral work operates without reference to visual aids of one kind or another, or without reference to a situational or topic-based framework, is often a mediocre lesson. The majority of children never find it easy to pay prolonged attention to words, words and more words issuing from the teacher's mouth or to the same words printed in a textbook. A lesson which lacks interesting visual material or demonstration with reference to concrete objects in the classroom cannot hope to gain and maintain the children's genuine interest. Their abject resignation easily becomes accepted by the teacher as a natural phenomenon of school life.

Besides stimulating the imagination and holding the attention a cartoon-type cineloop can bring movement and humour to the lesson. Slides or filmstrips can be informative as well as attractive: they can bring home to the pupils in a forceful way distinctive features of the foreign civilisation. The use of figurines and of quickly drawn pin-men and sketches on the blackboard can often clarify concepts and help to weld the essential bond that needs to be established between objects, qualities and actions and the linguistic unit which refers to them. Not only do good, colourful visuals enhance motivation, but, when specially designed, they also help towards more long-lasting retention of the corresponding piece of language. Visuals should not figure as mere addenda or luxury supplements to the language teaching business: they have a specific rôle to play in teaching clearly defined segments of language.

Since there seem to be a number of good reasons why tape-recorders, language laboratories, slide projectors and other pieces of mechanical and electronic equipment should be used in language teaching, it is pertinent to ask why they sometimes lie idle. What reasons are given by teachers for not using these valuable aids?

The first reason why these aids may not be fully utilised in schools where they exist is a very simple one: the teacher feels that he lacks both the competence and confidence to handle and operate the particular item in question. In the case of a full-scale audio-active-comparative language laboratory it is easy to take fright at the seemingly complex controls, but growing acquaintance will show that their operation is not so difficult as one might at first imagine. Much skill is, of course, required to get the most out of such equipment and the teacher needs to become familiar with the practical working of a language laboratory by attending talks and conferences, studying books on the subject and practising on the actual equipment in his own time. The challenge is worthwhile. In the case of a tape-recorder, a cine-loop projector and a filmstrip or slide projector, operation is not difficult. The essentials have to be learned, however, and practice on one's own when children are not present is something which is vital to success. After some initial instruction to selected individuals it is possible to get 'monitors' to operate projectors. Sometimes such 'monitors', when well trained, can manipulate projectors more skilfully than the teacher himself.

A second, more justifiable, reason for not using the mechanical items of equipment mentioned above is that much time can be wasted and trouble incurred in transporting and setting up. This is a real practical problem that cannot be brushed to one side. Part of the solution is for the Head to see to it that a room or rooms are allotted for the specific purpose of language lessons where possible so that audio-visual equipment remains in fixed positions. Trolleys and special covers, adjustable stands, extra ready-loaded slide magazines and filmstrip holders, pull-down screens, provision of electrical points and easily-drawn curtains or other forms of blackout are necessary, rather than luxury items. Teachers need to draw up detailed lists of the items they require and press for their acquisition through their Head of Department. Headmasters and Language Advisers are often able to draw on L.E.A. special funds where the teachers argue their case in writing and state with precision what items they require. The department may not get all it wants but it is likely to get more than it would have done if it had accepted an unsatisfactory state of affairs.

A third reason is also of a practical nature and demands our closest attention. Mechanical and electronic items of equipment are always subject to breakdown failure and every measure should be taken by relevant authorities to deal with this problem. Even a single headset not functioning properly can throw a lesson out of gear: extra spares of such items as headsets and projector bulbs are again essential. The services of a teacher who is also a qualified audio-visual aids technician are available in some schools: such full-time appointments should be argued for in all schools. Not until we have this technical assistance can we adequately cope with the servicing, repair and maintenance of equipment, and minimise the problems which constantly beset teachers trying to come to terms with technological change. Where a technician is not available the teacher can at least do his best to take care of equipment. He can make sure that the children handle headsets gently, that tape-recorders have dust covers, that hot projectors are not moved until they cool down, that tapes are kept in polythene bags and that their boxes are kept away from cold or damp and the heat of radiators, and so on.

All the practical problems associated with the use of mechanical items of equipment need our closest attention, but they should not be quoted to justify a disdainful attitude toward audio-visual aids in general nor to veil an unwillingness to learn how to exploit such aids. Difficulties need to be viewed in a spirit of challenge rather than of aggravation, since only in this light will they be solved.

None of the reasons examined above applies to the use of those items we have listed as non-projected visuals, all of which are quite simple to manipulate. It is, however, necessary to stress that objects and toys, flannelgraph figurines, posters and cards, require some time to set out ready for immediate use in a particular lesson. They also need to be well organised and prepared so that the lesson gets off to a smooth start during the first minute or so. If they are kept in clearly marked folders and boxes which are methodically arranged on the shelves of a cupboard at the front of the room, then they will be ready for immediate use. They can be grouped according to topic (the house, modes of transport, clothes, etc.) or according to the units and lessons of the particular course being used (Longman's Audio-Visual French, Stage 2, Unit 15, *Sous la tente*). This small amount of preparation, however, does not constitute an argument for not exploiting such visual material to the full. Especially with younger children good visuals serve to shift the focus of attention from the teacher to objects, actions, events and situations which give meaning and context to the words and sentences being heard by the children. Far too many lessons are given in which no contextual framework is provided for the sentence patterns and vocabulary being taught. Effective learning and retention are always impaired when there is a lack of semantic coherence and a referential framework for the segments of language being taught.

It is sometimes mistakenly thought that using visuals slows down the language teaching process, and too often we hear some teachers trying to justify their neglect of such aids by arguing that the syllabus has to be covered within a given number of years. Dispensing with visuals in an attempt to cover a greater area of language can do nothing but harm, especially to pupils who lack concentration or who have limited powers of absorption and retention. Using visuals does not slow down the pace of the total course, but rather leads to more thorough learning and to more effective long-term retention. Demonstration with objects and visuals in the early stages of language teaching provides a secure basis on which to forge in subsequent stages links between word-groups and clauses within sentences. At all stages, however, the associative links between language and the external realities to which it refers are all-important in the learning process.

13

In terms of time-economy such an aid as the overhead projector can prove to be of the utmost value. Its projected image is usually bright enough for it to be used in conditions where there is no black-out. This simplifies integration with various classroom activities. In a thirty-five-minute lesson some teachers can spend ten minutes or more writing material up on the blackboard. Most of their lesson time can be spent laboriously copying up a passage in the foreign language, a series of questions, correct answers, a dictation passage, sentences to be converted in one way or another, examples illustrating a grammatical point, phrases and idioms, elaborate maps, charts, drawings, and so on. The limited time that language teachers have needs to be used wisely for those matters that pupils cannot profitably undertake outside the classroom. Not only is precious time wasted in putting material on the blackboard during the lesson, but also time is wasted by pupils who can often copy into their exercise-books at a faster rate than the teacher can write up the material.

The teacher's engagement at the blackboard will often give some pupils the chance to sit back, to chat with their neighbour and generally to lose interest in the meaning and purpose of the material being dealt with. The work being done by the pupils, moreover, is usually of that kind which can be done just as easily for homework or private study. A given passage, a series of written questions or correct answers, the exemplification of a grammar point, the drawing of sketches, maps or charts, can nearly always be carefully prepared before lessons on acetate transparencies to be illuminated on the overhead projector at the appropriate moment in the lesson. Points arising during a lesson can easily be illustrated on the blank acetate scroll. The continuous scroll (where it runs in a North-South direction) allows rather more material to be presented than is possible in a few single transparencies. The limitation in the amount of written material that can be put on a single transparency is often an advantage, however, since it forces us to consider one point at a time rather than allowing us to overcrowd our lessons with too much material.

In terms of good presentation of properly prepared material

and in terms of time-economy this technique of projecting both textual and visual matter allows the teacher more time to operate effectively with the children. He is allowed more time to conduct intensive oral practice with individuals who need it, and he is in a better position to supervise the children's written work by walking round the class checking. The projected images of the transparencies on to a central screen act as an excellent focal point in oral work. The imaginative use of overlays greatly enhances this process.

With textual work answers can be shown beneath the questions which are on the basic mount, corrections or comments can be added to a dictation, points can be presented in turn or expanded by use of several overlays, sentences can be covered and then revealed one by one while oral question work takes place on each. A series of small pictures can be revealed in turn for oral composition work, a number of visual overlays can help to build up scenes from a central object on the basic mount, the colour of objects can be changed by means of a revolving disc-type transparency, profile shapes can help oral question-and-answer drill to become a guessing game. All such visual material will be carefully structured in accordance with linguistic principles, each step serving as the stimulus for the oral practice of a specific segment of language.

An added advantage of using overhead projector transparencies as opposed to putting material on to the blackboard is that the material does not have to be rubbed off at the end of the lesson. The elaborate map or chart, the questions, that brilliant clarification of a grammar point, remain for posterity, or at least for revision purposes or for another class of the same level.

Even less common than seeing the teacher make effective use of audio and visual aids is seeing the children themselves participating actively in some part of the process. In respect of the language laboratory it is of course essential for the children themselves to learn how to handle the equipment and make the best use of it. In lessons where use is made of the filmstrip or slide projector, an able and responsible member of the class can be instructed in its operation while the teacher is left free to operate the pause control of the tape-recorder. With regard to transparencies to be put on the overhead projector it is possible to involve a few children from the class. Selected individuals, for example, can write their dictations, or answers to questions, or oral compositions, on sheets of cellofilm. These will then be projected for class viewing and receive correction and comment. This procedure can allow for repetition of structures and vocabulary while at the same time maintaining interest through the display of work by different individuals.

With younger children not only will cellofilm be useful at that stage when writing is undertaken but also it can be used by selected individuals for drawing and picture work. The teacher gives a whole series of instructions in the foreign language using sentences familiar to the class. These instructions involve drawing and colouring various objects and setting them down in certain positional relationships: a black cat in front of the third tree, three birds on a branch of the second tree, two red apples on the ground near the first tree, number thirty-eight on the door of the house, a man with hat and umbrella, and so on. The possibilities are infinite. While correcting the efforts of those pupils whose aural comprehension test is being projected on the central screen, the teacher has further opportunities of repeating the necessary sentences and vocabulary or of doing further question-and-answer work to evoke correct answers from individuals in the class. Repetition and consolidation of segments of language are secured while interest is maintained.

Classroom objects, toys and flannelgraph figurines can be manipulated by at least some children for some of the time in a carefully organised lesson. The actions performed by individuals with the objects or figurines need to be integrated in a precise manner with the segments of language being practised orally. Verb forms may well include various persons of such easily demonstrated verbs as touching, taking, putting, picking up, choosing, passing, turning over, keeping, changing, showing, dropping, looking, asking, telling, and so on. These verbs will be practised in sentence contexts in conjunction with such prepositional phrases as: on the table, under the box, near the door, in your pocket, with your right hand, on his left shoulder. As we pass from real objects to figurines representing a multiplicity of absent

16

objects and from classroom situations to the unlimited world of imagined situations, we find once again that the possibilities are infinite.

Not only is it possible for selected children to manipulate those non-projected visuals usually reserved for the teacher's use, but also they can be provided with individual sets of visuals. Use of banda sheets with picture stories, packs of picture vocabulary cards and work-cards with picture cues can embrace all members of the class. The use of individualised visuals to a specific linguistic purpose requires a good deal of preparation and organisation. Picture stories may form the visual cues for graded question-and-answer work and vocabulary pictures can form the basis for various game-like drills conducted along 'bingo' lines, matching picture objects with the oral stimuli given by the teacher. Scope can also be given for some creative responses by the children if certain elements of a given series of pictures have to be inserted. Question-and-answer work based on individual banda pictures can be combined with the drawing and colouring work already described as an aural comprehension test.

If the teacher wishes to take a critical look at his own work in the classroom it is useful for him to ask at the end of a given lesson:

Did I use any audio aid apart from my own voice?

Has the tape-recorder or laboratory been put to good use?

Exactly what visual aids, projected or non-projected, have I used?

What actual materials and equipment have I or the children handled?

How many individuals have participated in handling and using different forms of visuals?

Such questions may well be more relevant to a series of lessons than to a single lesson, and they may be relevant especially to younger or less able groups of children, but whatever the circumstances if the answers are mostly negative then something is sadly wrong with the teaching. To say the least it will certainly lack interest and fail to stimulate the learners.

3
Providing a Varied Diet

Owing to the obvious pressures of teaching several classes per day it is all too easy for the unwary teacher to lapse into the habit of doing the same type of work throughout a thirty-five-minute lesson. Through lack of preparation time and other practical difficulties it is easy to adopt a fairly narrow repertoire of procedures which after ten to fifteen minutes begins to make for a rather monotonous lesson. The lack of variety in the form of work coupled with this limited mode of operation leads often to a general feeling of indifference and apathy among many pupils. Most will find their concentration waning before the middle of the lesson and some will develop a positive dislike for foreign-language study.

The exact nature of the form of work undertaken and of the type of techniques used is not the point at issue. The fault under discussion is not related directly to either materials or methods, since we may discover instances of it in any kind of lesson, whether this be along traditional or progressive lines. It is worth while, therefore, to give some examples.

The teacher may read several paragraphs aloud from a reader. He then gets various children to read a paragraph in turn. A few questions in the foreign language, sometimes in English, may be put to the class. Then the whole process is repeated with the next page, then again with the next and the next. This procedure requires little thought and preparation and usually takes everybody safely from the beginning of the lesson to a long-awaited moment thirty or so minutes later. The discomforts which might occur in the interim period we shall not dwell upon.

18

It is sometimes the case that a teacher deals with actual objects and uses them to teach a given grammar point, such as the various forms of the partitive article, the forms of the possessive adjective, the feminine agreement of adjectives (especially the irregular forms), the difference between '*il fait chaud*' and '*il a chaud*', the comparative and superlative, the use of '*qui*' as opposed to '*que*', the persons of an irregular verb like '*boire*', and so on. He may very well be a keen and knowledgeable exponent of the oral method. Having established through demonstration the meaning of the provisions placed on his table the teacher will then ask the class questions in the foreign language. The trouble is that only one type of simple basic question is used again and again. Usually these are questions beginning with '*Qu'est-ce que*', '*Qui*', '*Où*', '*De quelle couleur*', '*Quelle heure*'. Forms like '*Est-ce que*' and '*Quel*' are absent from the repertoire (see Chapter 8 for examples of the range of forms). The teacher's knowledge of all the various ways of formulating different questions is severely limited. Sometimes exactly the same question is repeated *ad nauseam* by the teacher and a kind of saturation point is achieved:

> *Qu'est-ce qu'il y a sur la table?*
> *Il y a du sucre, de la confiture, etc.*
> *Qu'est-ce qu'il y a sur la table?*
> *Du sucre, de la confiture, etc.*
> *Qu'est-ce qu'il y a?* (repeated)

Certain pupils will appear particularly obtuse by still offering an inaccurate or incorrect answer.

A third instance of pressing too hard for too long with the same kind of activity and a very restricted repertory of techniques is that kind of lesson which centres on the teaching of a grammatical point to such an extent that all meaning is lost. The significance of the 'message' carried by the linguistic units is entirely neglected. This kind of lesson concentrates on 'hammering home' a particular grammar point. Sometimes this is done with an extravagant use of explanation in English and a prodigal use of translation and analysis. Often the piece of grammar in question is not demonstrated with sufficient examples and is presented *in vacuo* without being contextualised or related to a visual framework. On the other hand the piece of grammar may be practised according to the most progressive oral and linguistic tenets, as we have observed in our second example in the preceding paragraph. Perhaps the whole lesson is in the booths of an audio-active-comparative language laboratory. One or more structure drills constitute the material of the lesson. The same stimuli and sentence patterns are repeated again and again, and the pupil gives his oral response to each stimuli, usually in a fairly mechanical fashion without too much attention to the meaningful content of what he is saying. The pupils then return to the beginning of the tape and work once again through the drill.

When a lesson is restricted to a single form of work or to the same exercise or activity, it is often the case that any initial interest on the children's part soon wanes. As the lesson proceeds the majority of the children find it more difficult to concentrate fully and they tire of the same pursuit. This is not to say that every lesson in which the class engage in the same type of work throughout is a bad one: variety within unity is quite possible, and sometimes the fault is offset by virtues possessed by the teacher in other directions. If some particular activity fires the imagination of the children, there is no reason why teacher and children should not follow it through for a whole lesson: organised project work with very young children can in the right conditions generate a good deal of interest and enthusiasm. We are not considering here, however, the exceptional teacher who is always able to stimulate the children and hold their interest. We are concerned more with the skill and craftsmanship required in teaching and building day by day the basic audio-lingual skills.

The weakness under consideration becomes even more sharply focused when we view a continuous sequence of lessons. The second and third lessons also contain a similar type of activity which is pursued throughout the thirty to forty minutes. The teacher seizes upon a fairly small number of types of work or exercise, the extent of which usually depends on the course or textual materials being employed. During the four or five periods available over the week he dwells with the class on each of the types of exercise and is constantly returning to each in ever-decreasing circles. It is not surprising, therefore, that pupils soon become aware of the teacher's restricted *modus operandi* and grow bored with it: familiarity breeds contempt, especially when the children realise that they are not progressing as well as they would wish.

Intensive oral work, either in the classroom or in the language laboratory, demands considerable effort from the children, especially when conducted at a swift pace as it should be. Such oral work, involving a good deal of repetition and question-and-answer work, should only be carried on for a limited time-span which is within the capabilities of the majority of children in the class. This time-span varies of course from pupil to pupil, from one age-group to another, from one ability-group to another, and even from one time of day to another, but for practical purposes it would not be far from the mark to say that with classes of younger children a period of fifteen minutes is ample for such concentrated practice.

The sensitive teacher who knows his pupils should be able to detect when class response is not so keen as usual, when the energies of certain individuals are at a low ebb, when fatigue is setting in, when pupils are sinking into lethargy through prolongation of a particular activity. At such moments there is a need to revitalise the work, to re-awaken the class, to re-focus the children's attention and interest. Switching to a new type of activity can often help to bring fresh zest and vigour to a lesson in which, aften ten or fifteen minutes, the children's energies are beginning to flag or their attention is beginning to wander.

The first measure to be taken by the teacher who wishes to guard against pursuing the same type of activity or exercise too long in a lesson is to prepare a more varied type of lesson by dividing his time into two, three, or four clear sections and by making a note of what he will do in each section. The second measure to be taken is to extend one's repertory of classroom procedures and techniques. Only if the teacher has an extensive repertoire at his fingertips will he be able to maintain interest and avoid a monotonous lesson. This knowledge of different techniques and the ability to manipulate them in class are not talents acquired casually through experience: knowledge and skill come by dint of hard work and study. The third measure to be taken in providing a varied diet is to view a given lesson within the context of three or four lessons and to see its place and function in relation to the series. Again it is a question of planning and preparation. It also involves knowing something about the various phases that constitute the language-learning process: presentation and demonstration, mimicry and repetition, structure practice, question-and-answer work, extension and exploitation, making free use of elements learned.

Dividing the lesson into two or more sections should not imply any lack of continuity. The first five minutes may well be spent on revision of a sentence pattern and a few vocabulary items learned in the previous lesson. This may perhaps be done through question-and-answer work with pupils doing most of the asking and answering. The next ten minutes may be listening to sentences on tape while looking at accompanying visuals: repetition and question-and-answer work may follow this for a further ten minutes, while the last ten minutes are spent on reading and writing work connected with the audio-visual work of the present lesson and of the previous lesson. Much depends, of course, on the level of attainment of the class. When the teacher knows how much his pupils have learned in previous lessons he should be able to devote a larger part of the time to re-working known words and word-groups into new sets of sentences, constantly keeping in circulation elementary linguistic units already learned.

Too often a teacher restricts the lesson to the viewing of a number of filmstrip frames where accompanying sentences are repeated by the children after they have heard them two or three times on tape. The work becomes drill-like and tedious. In the following lesson the whole thing is repeated but this time without so much repetition and with more question-and-answer work. The lesson after this is spent reading exactly the same material as has been dealt with orally, and then writing answers to the questions already practised orally. And so one proceeds, bit by bit, each lesson concentrating on a few segments of language, and the children go through each unit following the same pattern of audio-visual and oral techniques and the same types of reading and writing exercises. No attempt is made to use in the course of lessons those linguistic units already conquered in former lessons. There is no development, no growth, no increased oral fluency: there is only an aggregation of linguistic units which are for ever fading away into a distant past.

If the teacher uses a whole variety of aids and techniques in a series of lessons over the week, this should not imply any lack of integration or linguistic objectives. The imaginative teacher will know many ways of inculcating a given sentence pattern and of teaching vocabulary: he will be able to approach the same linguistic matter from many angles, knowing many kinds of game-like activities for teaching certain points. The same words, phrases, idioms and grammatical patterns recur in many different contexts and situations. While the language remains the same the activities and the kind of visuals used change from moment to moment: to the children the lesson appears to be varied because their attention is focused on the different activities, games, approaches and materials used, but what they are doing in fact is repeating the same segments of language. This repetition of the same patterns and vocabulary is not obvious both because of the variety in approach and activity and because the new linguistic units are unobtrusively embedded and practised in material already learned. The simple questions asked in the early stages of teaching recur, but they recur in amplified form with adverbial phrases of time and place tagged on to them, with noun phrases extended with adjectives and adjectival clauses, with subordinate clauses, with various clichés inserted, and generally with all kinds of 'padding' provided by previous lesson units.

Many teachers have some awareness of the phases of language learning which involve presentation by audio-visual means, followed by explanation, imitation and repetition by pupils, general question-and-answer procedures and structure drills, and oral reproduction. This awareness helps them to plan lessons and sequences of lessons so that some variety is afforded through proceeding methodically from phase to phase. Too few teachers, however, have a command of techniques relating to the further phases which figure under such headings as follow-up work, exploitation, transposition, activities, open conversation with novel utterances, and so on, which have to do with actually using the language learned in situations that closely simulate reality. The dramatic acting out of dialogues using real props and demanding personal involvement of the pupils is a difficult task, but this kind of exploitation work is an essential phase of the language teaching business: it is especially relevant where young children are concerned and can give additional help in the matter of providing a varied diet. Game-like activities and songs that are used to practise specific linguistic units can, when well organised, provide stimulating fare if they are introduced at the right moment in a lesson that involves intensive effort. Enjoyment is a legitimate objective to strive for.

In the fourth or fifth year of foreign-language study when pupils have begun to master the skills of reading and writing the language, it is possible to obtain a varied diet within the lesson period by shifting from one skill to another. A short narrative passage might first be presented on tape for aural comprehension. A series of pictures illustrating the story might then be provided on banda sheets for each pupil. Question-and-answer work may then ensue. The printed passage is then read in conjunction with teacher and tape, and then the outline only is provided for written reproduction. If the teacher is going to pass from one activity to another in this way, it should be noted that the passage will be limited to only a small number of sentences, illustrating perhaps one or two grammar points in context. A following lesson may well allow the pupils to perform varied substitution, transformation and expansion exercises on the same sentences. Although we have not gone into detail here it should be obvious that a lesson along these lines is more varied and interesting, and probably much more effective, than a lesson where one pupil after another reads aloud a paragraph from a reader and this form of work continues throughout the half-hour. And once again we may note that switching from one skill activity to another to provide variety does not of necessity mean a disin- tegrated lesson: with careful forethought and planning the lesson can have a central theme, a continuity of subject-matter and clearly defined linguistic objectives.

The failure to provide a varied diet within a lesson period and within the weekly programme comprising four or five lessons points to a lack of organisation and preparation on the teacher's part. It also points to a paucity of diversified techniques and interesting materials. Basically, however, it reflects a disregard for the ways in which individuals in the class learn. As we have noted, there are various remedies for the fault we are examining according to the specific nature of the shortcomings mentioned in our examples. In order to detect his shortcomings so that he may be able better to analyse his own situation, the teacher will find the following questions particularly relevant:

Did I press too long on one kind of activity throughout the lesson?

Have I used different materials and aids with the same class over the week?

Have I divided up the lesson into different types of work?

How many specific procedures and techniques were used in that lesson?

What balance am I achieving between the different skills?

What balance am I achieving between the various phases of the language teaching process?

How much spoken language acquired in previous lessons have I worked into this lesson?

It is not difficult for a teacher to fall into what appear to be easy routines. Over a period of time his *modus operandi* becomes excessively restricted and there is an undue emphasis on one or two types of exercise and activity. In such cases a consideration of the above questions should help to revitalise his work in the classroom.

4

Involving Children in Activity

In the first chapter we reviewed the teacher-dominated lesson in which nobody listens to what pupils have to say or even allows them to say anything in the foreign language. In this chapter let us go a little further into the matter and deal not just with the lack of an oral response on the part of individuals but with their obvious need to be involved in an active way.

Many teachers go to some pains in presenting the material and in demonstrating meaning through objects and visuals manipulated at a central focal point at the front of the classroom. In many cases the teacher expends a good deal of energy and performs effectively. During the question-and-answer interchanges the teacher may show considerable skill in getting oral responses from many individuals within the class. In spite of the fact that the teacher takes much upon his own shoulders and shows drive and energy, in spite of the fact that audio-visual aids are used, and in spite of the fact that oral responses are obtained from many individuals, there often still seems to be a something that is lacking.

Even though pupils imitate various sentences and give answers to questions, they still remain physically passive for all lessons. Experienced teachers know that it is not enough that they themselves should work hard: the pupils have to work hard too. A major part of the teacher's art and skill lies in getting them to do this under their own motivation. Force of circumstance, however, often leads pupils into playing a rôle akin to that of puppets or trained animals whose every response remains under the overt control of the handler. Such a situation is not always easy to avoid in many schools: large classes, reluctant learners, poor teacher-pupil relationships, an enforced externally imposed discipline, teachers inadequately trained, and so on, certainly do not create a flexible framework in which pupils can be allowed a high degree of freedom of movement, of action, and room for developing their responsibilities and using their initiative.

Far too common in our foreign-language classes is the lesson in which not a single pupil engages in any kind of physical movement which causes him to perform some action. The children have no opportunity to point to anything, handle anything, or do anything that involves standing up and moving their limbs. Stuck to their chairs they remain mere spectators of a game which involves no movement. Language learning is confined to looking, listening and speaking, with no regard whatsoever for doing anything. Somebody who has already acquired a language may well communicate without gesture or physical movement: this is the ultimate purpose of language. When language is first to be learned, however, physical activity may well play a more vital rôle than we suspect. Language not only symbolises a static world of objects but also relates to a constant movement of people and things.

Just as the associations between names and objects (or visuals representing objects) help towards the retention of meanings, so too the associations between words and corresponding actions help towards the same end. If a pupil can actually perform the action he is talking about while he is talking about it, learning will be that much more effective. Present conditions in our language classrooms do not lend themselves to the exploitation of this precept. Many teachers of older children in particular would shudder at the thought of children leaving their seats to perform some action or other. There are many schools in which such movement is only to be interpreted in terms of disruption. Teachers of physical education, however, would obviously have a rather more sympathetic attitude to such a suggestion. There are also many teachers of younger children, including language teachers, who already go some way towards creating an atmosphere and framework within the classroom which enables them to involve a number of individual children in activities of a physical nature.

If more than one pupil is to be out of his seat at one time, then the teacher will need to have already secured the co-operation and the goodwill of his class. As well as good class control the teacher will also need to be well organised and well prepared. To become an accomplished operator in such matters the teacher must develop specific techniques and procedures which he applies in a methodical fashion. If pupils are not to become restricted in movement and trapped in the narrow confines imposed by the passive type of lesson, then scope must be given for controlled and guided responses carefully programmed by the teacher. Although the actions and the utterances of the pupils are controlled by specific teaching procedures, the fact that they are controlled is not too apparent to the children themselves. The situational framework created by the teacher and the oral stimuli provided by him allow sufficient flexibility for activities not to become too rigid and stereotyped. Open-ended action drills in which the individual pupil has a choice of response have to be cultivated as part of the teacher's repertoire of procedures. They must always operate, however, as the final phase of a series which includes the more basic work of imitation, recognition, reproduction and manipulation work.

In our discussion of audio and visual aids in Chapter 2 we have suggested various ways in which individual children can be involved in handling equipment, different kinds of visual and performing appropriate actions. Especially with younger children it is possible to invite the pupils' participation during most phases of the language teaching process. It is not only during those parts of a unit coming under the heading of exploitation and activities that the children can be doing something more than just listening, repeating and answering oral questions.

During the demonstration phase of a lesson in which the teacher is presenting the meaning and exemplifying the use of a new sentence pattern or vocabulary item, it is nearly always possible to invite the co-operation of one or two individuals or even the whole class. There are many instances of vocabulary

28

and grammar points which are more effectively learned when they do involve some small activity, gesture or movement carried out by individuals from the class. Take, for example, a point I have seen taught many times rather poorly merely because the teacher relies entirely on his own abilities to demonstrate: the use of the French forms '*celui-ci*' and '*celui-là*' and related feminine and plural forms. It is not good enough to hold one book in the right hand, and then to distinguish between the use of the '*-ci*' form as opposed to the '*-là*' form. In such cases ambiguity often leads to confusion in the minds of the children and exasperation in the teacher, who soon laments the shortcomings of any direct-method type of approach. Let us examine this particular point in a little more detail since it illustrates a general principle of teaching technique.

The first job for the teacher to do in this particular case is to sort out the relationship between a number of related grammar points. The demonstrative adjective '*ce*' and its forms would need to have been established already. The forms '*-ci*' and '*-là*' may well be taught in relation to nouns referring to classroom objects: '*ce livre-ci est rouge; ce livre-là est bleu*'. The demonstrative pronouns '*celui*', '*celle*', etc. will probably need to be taught separately from the forms '*celui-ci*', '*celle-là*', etc., perhaps in a context relating them to 'possession': '*voici les vélos des enfants: celui de Jean est bleu; celui de Marie est noir*'. Each grammatical point needs to be considered in turn and the teacher will need to map out over a number of lessons the best sequence in which to deal with the points. The programming of this sequence does not mean that the points will be taught in successive lessons: in this case it may well be better to have a number of intervening lessons dealing with other material, otherwise the forms become confused in the minds of the learners.

Having sorted out the programming of the various points the teacher will find that many of his problems have already been solved. When teaching the uses of '*celui-ci*', '*celle-là*', much of the ground will perhaps have been covered since the children would already be familiar with the two parts that make up the combination '*celui-ci*' and its various forms. However, let us keep to our example in which the teacher is demonstrating the idea of 'this-near-me' and 'that-over-there'.

The teacher needs to hold up the object he is referring to so that everyone in the class can see it clearly. The other object of the pair needs to be placed away from the teacher but it still needs to be placed high up so that it is visible to all. The demonstrating can then proceed: '*Voici un livre jaune; voilà un livre rouge. Deux livres . . . un . . . deux* (pointing to each in turn). *Celui-ci est jaune; celui-là est rouge*'. Notice in passing that the distinction between '*voici* . . .' and '*voilà* . . .' involves the same point. Therefore the distinction may well be acquired in that context in the initial stages of language learning. The amalgamation of '*celui*' and '*-là*' would then present less difficulty to the learners. It is at this juncture that selected demonstrators come to the front or centre of the class and perform the same action: holding up and showing the yellow book and then pointing clearly to the red book. The pupil must look purposefully at the thing he is referring to and his gestures must be performed clearly and confidently; cultivating these aspects is an important part of the teacher's work. No time-wasting is to be tolerated, and if actions are performed quickly and boldly it is possible for a number of children to come to the front in turn. Two pupils can be used at a time if one of them does the speaking while holding the yellow book and the other stands across the room holding up the red book. The pupil with the red book can then be the speaker so that rôles are reversed.

While pupils are changing places the teacher will exploit the situation by speaking in French to the individuals and to the class as a whole, using sentence patterns and vocabulary they are acquainted with in the manner of a running commentary: '*Maintenant, c'est Jean qui va indiquer la différence. Il va montrer les objets d'une manière précise avec un geste. Oui, un peu plus haut, c'est ça, très bien. Parle à voix haute, je n'entends pas*', etc. The procedure of employing a number of demonstrators should be extended in two ways: by getting further verbal interchanges from pupils in the class, and by using a number of other objects and visuals in conjunction with different qualities. For example, a figurine depicting an elephant can be passed

30

round the class to be compared with a larger elephant on the blackboard or screen. The individual pupil holds up and points to his figurine, and then to the one at the front: '*Il y a deux éléphants: celui-ci est petit, celui-là est grand*'. At this stage we have discreetly entered the imitation and repetition phase of our work.

Substitution exercises and more creative responses can also involve some amount of participation on the part of individual pupils. For example, each pupil draws quickly on a piece of paper three classroom objects and when called upon by the teacher gives his oral responses: '*Voici une fenêtre* (pointing to his drawing); *voilà une autre fenêtre* (pointing to real window). *Celle-ci est petite, celle-là est grande*', and so on with the other two objects. This type of exercise must first deal with masculine forms and feminine forms separately before mixing them.

Question-and-answer work will consolidate the point and relate the new forms to the question words '*Quel . . .?*' and '*Lequel . . .?*' and to new situations: '*Quel chapeau préfères-tu? Laquelle de ces deux autos veux-tu?*' At all phases of the teaching process there is room for at least some pupil participation. However slight the activities and gestures performed by pupils may seem they should never be despised, since they can often provide a controlled starting-point for an extension to more busy activities like miming and acting out various rôles.

When teaching younger children, the verbs offer many opportunities for mime and action work. The teacher can ask individuals to stand up, to raise their left arm, to clench their fist, to show three fingers, to come to the front, to go to a map and point to towns and rivers, to look at the ceiling, to pick up various objects from the table, to open a window, to close a door, to crouch down, to turn round, to cross their arms, to indicate parts of the body and clothes, to write or draw on the board, to take a step to the right or to the left, to open a book, to pass a figurine to somebody, to change places with another pupil, to sit down, etc. The possibilities are unlimited. Two or three orders can be combined. Two or three pupils can be involved, and later a whole group may be acting out a prepared conversation and playing rôles in different situations: buying a drink in a café, getting a ticket at the station, buying provisions in a shop, asking the way somewhere, answering a telephone call, and so on. The key to success in rôle-playing lies in the teacher's skill in moving progressively over a period of months from directing a single pupil in a small action to controlling limited groups in more open-ended situations. Good preparation and careful organisation are essential, and there needs to be a growing mutual trust between teacher and pupils within the class.

There are, of course, many shy pupils who hate being called upon to perform in front of the class. Any interest that the reserved and reticent children may have in the foreign language can easily change to resentment if they are pressurised by the forceful extravert teacher. With such children the teacher needs a good deal of sympathy, understanding and tact. The teacher can help these children to overcome some of their shyness if he makes lavish use of encouragement and praise. By such means they develop a feeling of success and find they can win the approval of the teacher in some simple aspect of the active use of the foreign language.

Action chains in which one or two pupils perform a series of actions can serve as a basis for class question-and-answer work practising the perfect tense and the future tenses in context. What the pupil has just done forms the stimulus for work in the perfect tense: what the pupil is going to do provides the framework for work in the future tense.

A selected boy and girl from the class can perform alternately a specific mime indicating a particular verb, and individuals can guess the verb: '*il regarde, elle écoute, il mange, elle boit, il lit, elle dort, il écrit, elle nage, il se lave, elle coud, il pense, elle bâille, il joue au tennis, elle joue aux cartes, il s'habille, elle se peigne, etc.*' An extension of this type of work is possible if one is called upon to guess the object of those transitive verbs being mimed: '*Est-ce que tu manges un œuf? Est-ce que tu manges un fruit? Est-ce que tu manges du chocolat? etc.*' Once the class have become acquainted with this kind of guessing game, it is quite possible to expand the basic verb form with adverbial phrases and suchlike: '*Est-ce que tu nages dans la piscine? . . . dans la mer? . . . dans la rivière?*' Certain stock phrases can be agreed upon each lesson so that the scope of this work can be built up over the weeks. Almost any linguistic unit and part of speech can be practised in such a context: '*Est-ce que tu lis un journal anglais? . . un journal français? . . . un journal espagnol? etc.*' The whole key to success in this elaboration of the basic action depends on step-by-step progression over a number of weeks carefully planned and programmed by the teacher. Any attempt to introduce a number of aspects in a single lesson results in failure.

Whenever children become conscious of the fact that they are receiving little opportunity to exploit the aural and textual material being presented in any active way, they become bored and inattentive. As soon as they come to realise that no demands are being made on them as regards using the language in an active situation, they lose the desire to respond with vigour and imagination; their creative powers become dulled. If children think that the world of dialogues, conversations, visual scenes, and so forth, is a two-dimensional one that does not really involve immediately their personal active participation, they will come to regard the foreign language as an object remote from their basic daily needs.

The acquisition of oral fluency in a foreign language requires a lack of inhibition and a growth of confidence in the individual pupil. Actually using language in simulated situations of a dramatic nature, especially with younger children, helps towards real appropriation, better attitudes, and sure retention. Children need to feel that their active participation in the lesson is vital, that their personal contribution is essential, and that they, as individuals, are a very necessary part of the language teaching business. If the learner is to progress swiftly in his mastery of the basic skills, he needs to be for ever conscious of the fact that language is not primarily a body of linguistic facts but a vehicle and medium which accompanies, refers to and directs other activities.

The teacher will be able to analyse the amount of pupil-activity in his lessons if he asks himself in a direct manner the following questions:

Exactly what activity have pupils engaged in while at their seats?

How many pupils came out of their seats during the lesson to perform some mime or action?

Could I have made use of one or two pupils at the front of the class to help me with the presentation of some point?

Could I have used one or two people to help in the question-and-answer work?

Have I made any attempt at all to begin to create a framework and atmosphere in which a few children can engage in acting out a short dialogue and in rôle-playing?

The skills required in controlling and guiding a lesson in which a number of pupils are performing activities out of their seats while furthering their progress in the language are of a high order. Such skills and techniques are not acquired overnight: they result from knowledge, experience, industry, intelligent application, and the will to succeed.

5

Consolidating Skills through Practice

To equate the task of teaching with the acts of telling and explaining belittles the considerable talents, skills and craftsmanship needed for the job. Imparting facts and giving explanations may form part of the teacher's work, but it should only form a minor part of the business of developing the listening and speaking skills. 'Practice makes perfect' is a hackneyed dictum, but it is surprising how often this basic truth is either neglected or forgotten.

There is sometimes a marked disparity between the amount of material 'worked through' and the amount really thoroughly acquired by the children. So long as the syllabus is covered, so long as the necessary grammar points and vocabulary have been dealt with, and so long as some pupils grasp it all, then it is assumed that progress is taking place. Experienced teachers know, however, that many children have limited capacities for remembering and reproducing what they grasp at the moment. Learning can be fleeting and unsure unless measures are taken to consolidate and reinforce sentence-patterns and vocabulary and to provide individual children with intensive practice.

Thorough mastery of the aural and oral aspects of language learning can only be gained if the individual pupil is exposed to numerous repetitions and required to repeat his oral responses a number of times. Oral proficiency is mainly concerned in the first place with the exercise of certain habits and skills, and sufficient practice must be given at every step. Without this practice many individuals will remain unsure. They will hesitate and falter when imitating or giving an oral response. They will make mistakes in intonation, pronunciation, grammar, vocabulary and meaning. Some will articulate too softly, half-heartedly, with a lack of confidence. Some will become apathetic, reluctant to respond. The joy and satisfaction of uttering a sentence in a foreign language soon diminish. As the term progresses the performance of more and more individuals worsens. When too much material is rather badly presented the pupil finds difficulty in retaining much of it and that part he can recall is reproduced inaccurately. Sooner or later he becomes confused. Instead of feeling that he has mastered the material he feels besieged by it.

If teaching is to be thorough and effective and learning is to be sure, then repetition by teacher, by tape and by pupils is essential. If retention is to be long-lasting, if individual pupils are to produce oral answers with confidence and enthusiasm, if each member of the class is to improve constantly on his oral performance, then every linguistic unit in the foreign language must receive its due amount of consolidation, reinforcement work and active intensive practice. This inevitably means not only a vigorous, colourful and striking presentation of the units being taught but also a great deal of repetition and imitation. There must be constant revision built into the language programme, and units need to occur again and again in varied contexts.

It is important to define very carefully what we mean when we say there is a need for plenty of repetition. Repetition of a grammar point in the form of numerous examples, repetition of the same small number of vocabulary items, repeated imitation of a phrase or sentence, several repetitions of a question by the teacher or of an oral answer by the pupil, can lead to disgust in the learner. Repetition, if allowed to become mechanical and meaningless, can be performed in such a way as to cause boredom and distaste. It is not repetition *ad nauseam* that is wanted, not the mere mouthing of words and sentences, but spaced repetition of a more subtle kind. Repeating the same phrase four or five times within the space of a few seconds soon leads to a bored reaction from pupils. With the advent of structure drilling in the

36

language laboratory, many teachers know only too well what the dangers of over-repetition are.

The more subtle kind of repetition we are advocating should be a built-in feature of any good language course. Structures and vocabulary items are repeated at regular intervals from lesson to lesson. The same linguistic units will occur in a number of different situations and in conjunction with a range of varied visuals. Also it is possible in question-and-answer work to grade the questions in such a way that each question is just a slight variation on the previous one. New vocabulary items will be taught in the context of sentence patterns that are already familiar, and new sentence patterns will contain only words which are already thoroughly learned. The same linguistic units will be treated from a variety of angles. Numbers might, for example, first occur in list form as single units, but they will recur with teaching the time and with simple arithmetic involving addition, subtraction, multiplication and, when the learner has reached a sufficient level of attainment, division. Numbers can also recur in lessons dealing with shopping and handling money, in lessons dealing with distances between towns in France, in lessons dealing with pupils' height and weight, in lessons dealing with measurement, and so on. Another example might be that vocabulary related to swimming and diving may appear in the context of material dealing with a visit to the swimming bath, and then later reappear in a situation concerning an excursion to the sea-side.

If sentence patterns, vocabulary and idioms are tied to one time, one place and one situation, rather than utilised over a wide field, the pupil soon finds that he has not really acquired and appropriated the language, and he will not be able to use it readily and easily in natural everyday situations outside the immediate and confined situation of the classroom lesson. Pieces of language need to be used and re-used again and again so that they become absolutely commonplace to the pupil. This vital need to keep linguistic units in constant circulation from day to day is often forgotten if one treats language teaching as the imparting of a body of factual knowledge rather than as the development of a number of skills.

37

Examples of poor technique and procedure are evident in classrooms where the teacher has failed to appreciate that language teaching is a skilled craft. Too often the teacher passes hastily from one point to another without ensuring that the majority of the class have understood the point and received practice in it. In audio-visual and oral work, for example, it is not good enough to allow the pupils to hear a sentence twice only and to assume they have understood and heard correctly. Repetition of the sentence by the whole class as they hear it from the tape does not mean that every individual is speaking with understanding. Some pupils will only be mouthing the words mechanically, some will be speaking half-heartedly and saying the sounds in a distorted and inaccurate pronunciation, some will not be opening their mouths at all.

What is necessary is that a number of individuals must receive personal attention and be called upon to repeat the sentence by themselves. Choral work may be useful in the initial stages of language teaching and in the presentation of new sentence-patterns and vocabulary, but individual follow-up is essential. What the teacher must do is to point to four or five individuals in turn: each pupil speaks the sentence. The class are then hearing the same sentence spoken a number of times by their fellow pupils, and it may be remarked in passing that some pupils are more observant of something said by their equals than they are of the same thing issuing from the tape-recorder or the teacher. It is essential, of course, that pupils should not copy the poorer models, and there are certain measures that can be taken to guard against the imitation of bad pronunciation. The teacher will always say the sentence himself at the beginning of the individual practice and he will insist that the children listen very carefully to the sounds and rhythms of the sentence. He will also insist that when the pupil repeats the sentence great care should be taken over these details. It is also a good idea to begin with brighter pupils who do have a good pronunciation so that others may follow their example. It is not necessary for the teacher to repeat the stimulus model before each pupil repeats, since this would slow the whole process down, make it boring and reduce the pupils' number of contacts with the spoken language in a single class lesson. It is useful, however, to repeat the stimulus model from time to time, say after every three or four responses.

So that a number of individual responses can take place in a short space of time, it is recommended that the teacher merely point quickly at the pupil who is to respond rather than name him. Oral interchange then flows a little better. Knowing the name of each individual is essential, and calling him by his name is a vital part of establishing a sympathetic relationship with him, but there are opportunities at other points in the lesson where the teacher can make use of names. It is necessary, however, to take care over certain matters of detail which we shall now examine.

First, even though the work proceeds at a fast pace, it must not appear too hurried and the teacher must really cultivate the ability to listen attentively to the individual pupil's effort. This is not easy when the teacher's eye has to be kept on the class as a whole, but the teacher must remember that the goodwill of a class depends on the goodwill of the individuals who make up the class. The teacher, in spite of the necessity to keep the class within his view, should endeavour to make clear that he is interested in the individual's response and is listening critically to it. Having listened to the response, the teacher may need to correct it. The way in which this is done is important. He must never appear to be angry or disappointed; encouragement will aid progress, but any signs of discouragement or disapproval can only destroy the learner's confidence. What the teacher does is to repeat the model sentence and direct the pupil's attention to that part of it that is being pronounced wrongly. He then passes to two other pupils, perhaps among the more able, who can give the required correct imitation or response and after this returns to the pupil who requires more practice of the correct response.

In order to facilitate the quick oral exchange between the teacher and a number of pupils it is a good idea for the teacher to move into the aisles of the class so that he stands nearer the individual pupils. In this way he can often hear the pupil better than when he stands at the front, and also, there is no mistake as to which pupil he is pointing at. It is also useful to keep every individual alert by distributing questions or model statements over the whole class. It is no good directing them at the front row only or at pupils who put their hand up. It is better to develop a habit of switching from one side of the class to the other, from the front to the back of the class, asking two or three pupils in one corner, some in the centre, and so on.

When an individual pupil does give a correct imitation or response the teacher must give some clear sign that it is correct either with an approving nod or by direct verbal encouragement. An expression of pleasure and a *'très bien'* by the teacher to individuals can do much to build up confidence in oral response. It is not enough, moreover, to utter indiscriminately *'très bien'* in automatic fashion to every answer and to every pupil. It must be accompanied by a look of satisfaction and be used when responses are clear and accurate. Children who are shy, who are resentful or who are continually failing will need rewarding for their efforts if they are to make any headway at all at an oral level. This personal encouragement is one of the key factors in establishing good relationships with a class and in getting pupils to feel they are making progress.

From the very first lesson the teacher needs to show pupils that he is not going to accept answers which are too soft. He must tell the pupil to speak up or he must put a cupped hand to his own ear to show the difficulty. High standards of oral response are set at the beginning of the course; if an individual pupil has to repeat his answer three or four times it does not matter so long as embarrassment is somehow avoided and a satisfactory response is achieved in the end. The point is that the teacher will have to live with half-audible responses for ever after if he does not secure what he wants at the beginning. The wear and tear on his nerves and the frustration of the class will become unacceptable.

From what we have said so far about the need for repetition, consolidation and intensive individual oral practice, it should be obvious that such an aid as the language laboratory, used skilfully with the right kind of prepared materials, can be of the utmost value. Even with a fairly simple audio-active type of laboratory the opportunity for all individuals in the class to speak a sentence or answer questions simultaneously saves a vast amount of time. Instead of dealing with each member of the class in turn, so that during fifteen seconds or so only one person is gaining speaking practice, the teacher is able to allow thirty pupils to voice a response. It is true that he can only listen to and supervise one pupil at a time, but if the material is well graded and pre-lab classwork has precluded the possibility of numerous errors, then the benefits are inestimable.

It is not necessary for me at this point to expatiate on the virtues and limitations of the language laboratory, since there are several good books and articles the teacher can read on this matter. My intention here is merely to emphasise that in his classwork the teacher needs in most cases to ask the same question more than once to several individuals. This will help towards more thorough teaching and better retention of the material being taught, since the necessary repetition will be assured, accuracy and fluency will be developed, pupil participation will improve, and the confidence of individuals will be strengthened, especially if praise is given for correct and clearly voiced responses.

The techniques we have been advocating in this chapter are at variance with the situation which obtains in some classrooms. What can often happen is that when the teacher puts a question to the class, some children put up their hand eager to answer the said question while many others will not wish to answer for one reason or another. One correct answer is accepted from one individual. There are always some individuals who have not even heard the question and the answer given, let alone understood the meaning of the question and answer. If the teacher then rushes hastily to the next question and proceeds in the same manner, a proportion of the class, be this proportion large or small, will remain unsure and will not have received one ounce of oral practice.

When several individuals are called upon to repeat the answer to a single question put by the teacher, it is essential in the initial stage of the course to inform the children why this is done. The children must be taken into the teacher's confidence and be told that the purpose behind asking the same question and getting the same answer a number of times is to afford and secure intensive individual practice and consolidate the linguistic units being learned. The course goals and objectives relating to oral proficiency must be made clear to the pupils themselves. Apart from correctness of utterance and accuracy of pronunciation, speed and fluency is important. There should be no unnatural slowing down of the utterances; they should be spoken quickly and surely at as near native speed as possible. If a pupil says a sentence in hesitant manner with a pause or pauses between words and phrases, the teacher should get him to say it again more quickly, and again if necessary until the sentence is uttered with a single flow from beginning to end. High standards of fluency are only gained through insistence and persistence on the teacher's part and perseverance on the learner's part.

In all question-and-answer oral work it is vital that a good pace be set. The questioning needs to proceed in a vigorous, brisk fashion, without any lingering on items. The pace should not be allowed to flag because some pupil cannot answer quickly; it is better to pass to other pupils who can answer and then return to the slower pupil.

At the end of a lesson containing question-and-answer and repetition work the teacher can consider his answers to the following questions:

Did I ask the same question to more than one pupil?

How many pupils were given the opportunity to repeat each sentence or answer each question?

Did I correct inaccurate answers and insist on quick fluent responses?

Did I get pupils to speak out clearly?

Have the majority of individuals received sufficient intensive oral practice of each bit of language taught in the lesson?

Is everybody in the class sure and confident about what he knows?

Thorough and effective learning depends on the adoption of specific techniques and procedures that allow for repetition, reinforcement and consolidation of speech patterns.

6

Creating a Lively Pace

We have now reached the half-way mark in our examination of foreign-language teaching at the shop-floor level. Throughout our analysis we have emphasised the adoption of specific techniques and procedures which make for a skilled and knowledgeable craftsman. Competence in the skills being taught, ability to use good teaching techniques, insight into the nature of language learning and the developmental psychology of children, are all basic to successful performance. We all know, however, that the whole tone and atmosphere of any given lesson is strongly conditioned by the personality of the teacher and the kind of relationship he has with the individuals within his class. Successful teachers usually stand out on account of their enthusiasm, vitality, patience, tolerance, friendliness, sympathetic nature and their desire to see children achieve their full potential.

Before proceeding to the second half of our study in language teaching techniques it is essential to stress these 'personal' qualities which colour the teacher's manner of approach. There is no doubt that aspects of 'personality' are often difficult to define and develop. However, many features are not quite so cryptic as some would have us imagine.

The dull lesson, the type of lesson in which children are uninterested and inattentive, is often characterised by a lack of genuine interest and vital enthusiasm on the part of the teacher. If the teacher finds himself in a slightly depressed, arrogant or aggressive mood children quickly recognise and react against such a manner. If the teacher raises his voice it can too often act as a challenge and bring resentment and truculence from the children. Moreover, if the whole pace of the lesson is slow and children are not kept constantly alert and busy by the material being dealt with, then there will always be some children willing to fill the gaps with behavioural problems.

Where the teacher works hard and proceeds at a brisk pace, and shows a genuine interest and enthusiasm in what he is doing, the lesson is usually more likely to be a lesson in which most children are eager to learn. If the teacher is also of a cheerful disposition and deals quietly and sympathetically with individual children, then the lesson is that much better. The mood of the moment coupled with the teacher's general manner are critical factors in the matter of class discipline, so at all times the teacher should be sensitive and alert to the needs of the day. The teacher's own energies and enthusiasm are of the utmost importance, since neither methods nor materials will make up for deficiencies in 'personal' qualities. Good personal relationships between teacher and taught lie at the root of all good learning situations.

In Chapter 2 where we discussed the use of visual aids we examined the complaint that visuals slow down the teaching process. We saw that this view is unjustified and that the use of visuals enhances motivation and leads to more effective long-term retention of the material being learned. The same kind of criticism is often voiced by some teachers against audio-visual courses in general. All too often, however, the fault lies not in the materials themselves but in the way they are used. Too many so-called audio-visual lessons lack pace.

The children watch the filmstrip and listen to the accompanying sentences issuing from a tape-recorder. Each frame or picture appears in turn and remains on the screen for some seconds while the childen listen to the utterances related to the picture. During the imitation phase the class and individuals repeat the sentences after the model. This work too often proceeds in a slow, methodic and mechanical manner and can be just as boring and tedious as a lesson in which textbook and grammar explanation are the main elements. It is often the case that the pauses on the tape in which the pupil is meant to give his imitation or response are too long. This is what partly contributes to the tedium since the pupil has to wait a short moment after he has given his answer before the next stimulus comes on the tape.

In both the presentation and imitation phases of audio-visual work with filmstrip and tape-recorder the stimuli and pupil responses should follow swiftly one upon the other in a continuous chain-like activity. It is essential to train pupils to produce immediate responses. Much preparation and practice are necessary before this quick give-and-take can take place. It is obvious that children need to be thoroughly familiar with the techniques involved. If an individual pupil has to imitate a particular sentence he should be trained to begin his utterance almost before the model stimulus has finished issuing from the tape. Gaps and pauses between stimuli and responses must be cut down to a minimum, and there should be no waiting for the next stimulus. Where the teacher inherits tapes which have rather long pauses pupils can try to fit in two repetitions of the response, whispering the first as a preparation for voicing the correct reply. This subvocal 'rehearsal' can often help concentration and can also benefit those pupils who become nervous or hesitant when speaking aloud.

Usually the individual frames or pictures on the filmstrip form a sequence and may be based on a continuous narrative or piece of dialogue. After the initial work on presentation and imitation there should be a 'revision' or 'consolidation' phase in which there are no pauses between the presentation of the frames on the screen. The dialogue or narrative is heard as one continuous unit while the corresponding frames appear quickly on the screen one by one without stopping on any one frame. This manœuvre requires that the taped dialogue or narrative is carefully recorded with this objective in mind. It also requires an able operator at the filmstrip projector. This 'consolidation' phase can be likened to a cinefilm with sound track, and indeed the cineloop could probably fulfil the rôle more effectively, but this would inevitably mean a duplication of the same material on filmstrip and cineloop and would be very expensive.

During the question-and-answer phase the same continuous chain-like activity should characterise the interchange of stimuli and responses between tape and pupil or teacher and pupil. This work should proceed at a good pace. For oral work to be effective in bringing into play the children's natural, spontaneous and unconscious powers of assimilation, it is necessary to make the question-and-answer work appear as it would in normal everyday conversation. If the pace of utterances and oral exchange is slow, the learner has not the faintest hope of achieving the goals of quick aural comprehension and oral fluency. Responses need to be prompt to the point of being automatic so that attention is focused as much as possible on what is said rather than on how it is said. If the learner is encouraged to think out answers with his analytic and synthetic powers and is always given time to consider consciously his responses, he will never reach that stage of mastery of the spoken language when message and meaning dominate the form of the sentence.

The utterance of basic linguistic units has to become second nature. This goal can be achieved only through familiarity with whole stretches of language comprising meaningful word-groups and clauses. Concentration on the sentence as a complete pattern of sounds, as a 'Gestalt', is more easily achieved where question-and-answer techniques are exercised at a good pace. If this question-and-answer work is well contextualised with good visuals and lively realistic situations and is carefully sequenced, the children's attention will be directed to the meaningful content of the sentences rather than to their linguistic structure, which will be assimilated in a more subtle and less conscious manner than is evident in many classrooms. Rapid comprehension and oral fluency become possible only at that stage in language learning when emphasis is on the matter and meaning of sentences rather than on the formal properties of the words they contain. To reach this stage the question of increase in pace is of the utmost importance, since it is precisely through the briskness of oral interchange that the pupils are compelled to think beyond the language used to the meaning of their utterances.

Question-and-answer work cannot be conducted at a rapid pace unless the questions are very finely graded. Every question needs to be carefully formulated and structured in such a way that the answer, or a large part of it, is already contained in the

46

question. A simple example will suffice here to illustrate the point.

If the linguistic unit '*il nage*' is being taught and practised, the children may well be looking at the picture of a boy swimming. After the presentation phase in which the teacher says the sentence while pointing at the picture and the children imitate, the questions put to individuals in the class might be graded in the following way:

1. *Est-ce qu'il nage?*
2. *Est-ce qu'il saute ou est-ce qu'il nage?*
3. *Est-ce qu'il nage ou est-ce qu'il saute?*
4. *Est-ce qu'il saute?*
5. *Qu'est-ce qu'il fait?*

These questions are graded in such a way that each question asked is slightly more difficult in form than the previous question. Questions 1 and 2 merely require that the pupil repeat the last thing said by the teacher, which is not much more than an imitation exercise. Question 3 requires that the pupil recognises the correct form from two alternatives. Question 4 requires a simple negative '*non*', followed by an optional production of '*il ne saute pas*' or '*il nage*' or both: '*Non, il ne saute pas; il nage*'. Question 5 requires that the pupil recalls, from the memory store, the correct verb form.

Quick oral responses will not be forthcoming from the less able pupils in the class if the teacher is continually putting Question 5 as a first and only question. Doing this will not afford much repetition practice of new and familiar forms either. This matter of grading questions is especially important with regard to the less able learner. The either-or questions serve as useful prompts and allow the teacher to maintain the flow of oral interchange. Maintenance of a good pace depends a great deal on this gradation of questions. Our remarks on this matter should also be related to what we have said in the previous chapter. It is also worth noting that at the intermediate and advanced stages of a course the grading of more complex questions is frequently entirely overlooked, sometimes in classroom circumstances where it could be of immense value.

Since good audio-visual courses have a built-in limitation of structures and vocabulary items presented in a gradual manner, it is all the more important to work rapidly as well as thoroughly. Our insistence on pace and meaning in presentation, imitation and question-and-answer procedures, however, holds good with whatever kind of course we use. The manner in which the teacher conducts the work is fundamental to his endeavours to motivate the pupils, to focus their attention on meanings rather than words, to secure the maximum number of pupil contacts with the language in any given lesson, and to give children a feeling of success in making progress. The right kind of rapid oral practice can make the language lesson a satisfying, and even exhilarating, experience.

The teacher who wishes to keep a watchful eye on the matters treated in this chapter is advised to give careful consideration to the following questions:

Am I injecting enough pace into the lesson?

Am I insisting that pupils respond quickly and fluently in imitation and question-and-answer work?

Am I achieving a natural flow in responses from one individual to another within the class?

Is the emphasis being put on meanings rather than on the form of sentences?

Are my questions carefully framed, graded and placed in correct sequence?

If a high standard is achieved by teacher and class in these essential aspects of technique and manner, then not only will pupils gain more contact time with the language but also experience a feeling of progress and growing mastery in speaking the language.

7
Developing Listening Comprehension

In the first chapter we examined the kind of lesson in which there is an excess of teacher-talk. The lesson in which pupils play merely a passive rôle can easily become the rule of the day. The reverse side of the coin, however, also has its dangers: the lesson where children are starved of exposure to a large amount of talk in the foreign language. Like all good teaching practice it is a matter of balance.

If children are to develop their powers of aural comprehension and subsequently attain a high degree of oral proficiency, they must receive abundant opportunities for hearing authentic speech spoken by the natives of the country at normal speed. They should hear a variety of male and female voices from tape and radio, and they need to hear narratives, dialogues, conversations, and so on, based on colloquial everyday speech patterns and vocabulary. The limitation of the classroom and the pressures of difficult practical circumstances often militate against hearing enough of the foreign language. Consequently children receive insufficient nourishment and are often starved of data on which their learning capacities can operate.

Some teachers need to make much more use of authentic speech models on tape and they need to speak much more in the foreign language themselves. To speak in English all the time is deplorable. Almost as bad, however, is the case where there is too strict a limitation on the amount uttered by the teacher and the amount of spoken foreign-language material presented in any given lesson.

49

Let it not be thought that starvation is always due to a lack of oral competence on the teacher's part. It is indeed true that some teachers become inhibited when it comes to talking naturally in the foreign language to their pupils in the classroom but it is also a fact that many a bilingual fails to exploit fully his oral command of the foreign language. A study of how children acquire language clearly shows that pupils bring certain mental capacities to the learning situation provided that the raw material on which these capacities can work is present.

One very useful indicator of lesson performance is the amount of the foreign language heard and understood by the children. In a general way this amount can be measured and quantified as a rough percentage of the total lesson time. It is not difficult to find cases where the percentage is absurdly small.

It is wisely advocated that the structures and the number of vocabulary items presented as new material in a single lesson should be controlled and limited. We are all aware of the need for careful graded presentation of a small number of new points to be thoroughly mastered before passing to yet more new material. Most courses reveal at least some acquaintance with the principles of programmed learning; they rightly sequence and grade the grammar and vocabulary so that the learner is not given too much to deal with at any one time. What needs emphasising, however, is that we are talking about new and unfamiliar material, not familiar learned material. There is no suggestion that the teacher should leave aside all oral use of what patterns and vocabulary have already been acquired by pupils in previous lessons and in previous terms.

Fluency in the spoken language comes from constant progressive practice over a period of many months and many years. Continuous endeavour in mastering a greater and greater area of language requires hard work and perseverance from the learner. The total process is a developmental one in which the learner gains more and more confidence in using basic sentence patterns and in manipulating words into an infinite variety of combinations. If we study the case of young children learning their mother tongue, we observe that every day they are using the same sentence patterns and certain stock sentences and phrases again and again.

It is evident that all the familiar items are kept in constant circulation, and at various points amid the welter of talk we have the weaving of new combinations of words.

Just as the pseudopodia of the amœba engulf particles of food, so too the mind of the child seizes useful new words and incorporates them into an existing familiar body of word patterns. Without continuous exposure to the speech of a given community the child would never learn the 'rules' for combining words into correct and acceptable patterns. Feedback from authentic models is essential for his linguistic development.

The language teacher should never allow the need for formality to lead to paucity of speech in the foreign language. Many situations, events and actions that occur in the lesson lend themselves to comment in the foreign language, yet frequently they pass unexploited. Some teachers fail to seize opportunities and seem not to think it worth their while to speak in the foreign language about something not directly concerned with the prepared lesson material. This is a wrong attitude, since it tends to regard language as an esoteric body of knowledge rather than as a natural vehicle for expression and communication of thoughts.

The conditions in which teacher-talk in the foreign language is most effective have been amply described in Chapter 1. There we stressed the need for it to figure prominently in the initial stage of language learning and in the presentation phase of any given unit of material. We pointed out the need to use visual material, appropriate mime and dramatisation, and to train pupils in listening and in recognising different purposes in different kinds of listening exercises. The need to check comprehension through question work and to control the linguistic content of teacher-talk has also been discussed. What we shall now enlarge upon are the ways in which a teacher can prevent his pupils from being starved of language in lesson after lesson.

In any given lesson the teacher needs to make use of what has already been mastered by pupils at an oral level. To create a French atmosphere and to make French a living language in the artificiality of the classroom, the least the teacher can do for his pupils is to use French in a natural manner and show them it is a normal means of communication and expression. The teacher must of course be constantly developing his own oral competence. Not only this but he must lose his inhibitions about saying things he might consider trivial, commonplace, trite or self-evident. In learning a foreign language in its spoken form no chatter is idle chatter; every exclamation, every comment, every remark and every piece of language uttered give children matter on which their powers of aural discrimination and listening comprehension can operate and develop. Passive absorption of pieces of language associated with appropriate situations, events and actions needs to precede attempts at gaining active oral fluency. It is only by hearing pieces of natural language repeated in context again and again that real assimilation of spoken forms will take place.

By example the teacher can show the children how every action and movement in the classroom, however incidental or accidental they may be, can provide an occasion for using some relevant piece of language. What the teacher can endeavour to cultivate is the habit of vocalising, of remarking on and describing what he is doing and what he is going to do at any particular moment in the lesson. He can also exploit linguistically what individual children are doing, what they are feeling, how they are reacting, naming what is being handled, what has happened and what might happen. In general a kind of running commentary needs to take place, and in order to facilitate this the rôle of visual aids used by teacher and children as detailed in Chapter 2 and the part played by pupil participation as described in Chapter 4 should be obvious. If the lesson is devoid of objects and visual materials and of movement and activity, the need for comment and description in the language also disappears. The teacher's talk should not be supplementary or something apart from the main substance or theme of the lesson, but rather should be woven into the general fabric of the lesson, flowing out from it at every point; activity and linguistic experience should go hand in hand, each feeding the other in turn.

It is useful for the teacher to build up his stock of '*phrases utiles*' for constant classroom use. From the initial stages of the language course a repertory of instructions and commands, of requests and exclamations, of warnings and counter-statements, can be built up in the foreign language. The classroom routines of monitors setting out materials, giving out work and books, pupils sitting and looking to the front, individuals helping the teacher to hold up visuals or to pass them round the class, taking figurines from the flannelgraph and putting them into envelopes; all such matters afford an opportunity to the teacher to converse and give instructions in the foreign language. There should be certain stock formulæ used for greeting the class and beginning the lesson and for taking leave of the class and ending the lesson. Asking the time, the day, the date, the names of pupils absent, the nature of the previous lesson, the state of the weather, can serve as useful introductory question material for any given lesson. Such preliminary question work should help pupils to adjust to the foreign-language lesson as soon as they enter the room.

When the lesson content is focused on reading and writing activities, the teacher can still issue his instructions in the foreign language, saying who is to read a given sentence, who is to continue with the next sentence or so, whether the pupil is to repeat a group of words, how he should correct certain aspects of pronunciation, which page the class should turn to, whether the class are to copy the questions as well as write answers, how many questions the class are expected to answer, whether the work is to be done on a fresh page, what various pupils have written in answer to a particular question, how many lines an individual has written in a composition, and so on.

When the teacher first begins to conduct matters in the foreign language, very simple commands and easily phrased questions will be the order of the day. After a few weeks, however, the actual wording of the questions, requests and commands, can become a little more varied and complex. After some months the teacher can continue to use the same basic formulæ, but add a substantial amount of extra 'padding' and subsidiary comment. The instruction will be understood by the pupils but it will be embedded in other linguistic items which afford practice in listening comprehension. This principle of expansion applies also to oral question-and-answer work where the class have progressed from the elementary to the intermediate and advanced stages of the language course: the simple, concise question becomes the augmented question; the augmented question becomes hidden between a couple of statements loosely connected with it.

To limit children to hearing a small amount of the foreign language spoken by a teacher who may not be orally very fluent and whose intonation, accent and pronunciation are far from perfect is to do them a grave disservice. Even when the teacher is bilingual or has a high degree of oral proficiency, it is not enough that he alone should be the model for all oral work. In the initial stage of language learning it is perhaps necessary to provide pupils with a single voice source so that they become adjusted and attuned to the correct intonation patterns and rhythms of spoken sentences. As soon as the learner feels at home with the foreign pronunciation, however, and has progressed some way in the course, he should be exposed to a wider and wider range of authentic native models emanating from varied audio sources such as radio, tape-recorder, record player, television.

At the intermediate and the advanced stages of aural comprehension pupils can listen to male and female voices, adult and children's voices, and deep and shrill voices. The pace of delivery can also vary from the slow and deliberate to the rapid and fleeting. The tonal qualities of the voices can be shrill, gruff, excited, and so on. In developing older pupils' comprehension of rapid speech we need to remember that not only do visuals and total context play an important rôle but also relevant sounds and noises. Whistling, barking, shouting, engines roaring, birds cheeping, wind howling, water splashing, fire crackling, doors slamming, footsteps on gravel, panting, crying, scratching, and a hundred other sounds and noises on a tape can all be important clues in deciphering the meaning of sentences within their situational context at an aural level.

When tape-recorders are used the quality of sound reproduction must be above reproach. The distinction between a French '*p*' and a French '*b*' is not easily discernible to the English learner, and so it is with many sounds in a foreign language: '*t*' and '*d*', '*peur*' and '*peu*', '*bon*' and '*banc*', '*le*' and '*leur*' are but a few examples to illustrate the point. Clarity and distinctness of utterance are essential and it is all too common in the class-

54

room to hear blurred and muffled sounds, sometimes quite distorted, issuing indistinctly from a poor quality tape on a cheap tape-recorder being used in bad acoustic conditions. This inability to get the best from a tape-recorder and use it in satisfactory conditions leads us to suggest that it is not wise policy to rely on it for the introduction of new language in the initial stage of the course. It is better for the teacher to rely on his own voice to begin with.

Audio aids such as tape-recorders are effective only if they are properly and sensibly used in satisfactory conditions. It is essential to ensure that the tape itself is good standard quality and that the tape-recorder meets a satisfactory level of technical specifications with regard to wow and flutter, signal to noise ratio, frequency response, bass and treble cut and lift tone controls, power output and so on. However, a tape-recorder which is less than first class may well be more acceptable with the provision of a loudspeaker. Most language tapes are produced for a two-track machine, but if a four-track machine has to be used, track 1 should be selected. Tapes not used for some months need to be given a fast wind-through at regular intervals in order to avoid the print-through which can develop. A cleaning kit for tape-recorder heads is a useful purchase, and if possible, the tape-recorder should be serviced at least at the end of each year. Since quality of sound reproduction is vital in oral work an extension speaker can be extremely useful and wherever possible should be fitted to the tape-recorder. At advanced stages of the foreign language course a good radio set can serve a useful function in the development of listening comprehension. At the beginning of a lesson as the children come into the room a radio broadcast in French can do much to create an 'atmosphere' and to help the class to adjust and prepare their mental 'set' in readiness for oral work.

We have already mentioned the merits of the language laboratory for listening comprehension when we discussed the need for consolidation and intensive individual oral practice. Every provision should be made in a school for individual pupils to attend at flexible times to hear at a booth with comparative facilities whole recorded passages of narrative, dialogues, playlets, conversations, followed by comprehension exercises of varied type. Open access of this kind is essential for advanced pupils and if carefully planned and organised a tape library system can also be made available to responsible pupils below Sixth Form level. The possibilities of portable cassette recorders for use by individuals we shall not embark on here, but the opportunity they offer for increased contact time should not be ignored.

A natural facility for understanding rapid speech as spoken by the French native and for attaining an automatic mastery of oral utterance is not gained just by making use of conscious capacities and by concentrating on carefully prescribed daily doses of new matter. We must endeavour constantly to bring into play the children's natural, spontaneous and subconscious powers of assimilating. We can never do this by continually restricting the amount they hear in the foreign language. Observation of young children learning a foreign language reveals that they are quick and eager to seize on the meaningful content of what is said, tending to regard the formal linguistic elements of the sentence as means to abstract the relevant concepts and the total meaning. With young children skill acquisition is not brought about by analytical techniques which break sentences down into separate parts. It is easier for them to grasp the significance of word-groups that embrace meaningful concepts than to juggle with the form of single words in attempts to decipher the message. To exploit this facility in young children of eight or nine years of age it is necessary to work at a brisk pace which compels them to focus attention on what is being referred to rather than on an analysis of the tiny bits that make up the message.

If the principle of subordinating the language to the activity is observed in practice, it will be found that more rapid progress is made in listening comprehension, and consequently in oral fluency. By a good use of description, definition, antonym, synonym, paraphrase, and exemplification in oral texts, within the foreign language, it is quite possible to build up an extensive vocabulary while keeping up a constant delivery of speech in the classroom. This oral activity can easily be integrated with the reading of texts at the intermediate and advanced stages of the language course. How often is the oral element discarded, however, when reading is the main activity being undertaken by the pupils! All too often a pupil is asked to read aloud a passage containing unfamiliar words and structures before he has even heard this passage read by the teacher or by a recorded voice.

The value of cultivating listening comprehension lies not only in preparing the way for oral fluency. It is justified as an important skill in its own right. Pupils will spend more time in their lives listening to the foreign language than in speaking it; it seems sensible to prepare them fully in the skill that they will probably need most. Less able learners, moreover, can often achieve more with this receptive skill than they can with the productive skill of speaking.

For any given lesson or week of lessons it is worthwhile examining the answers to the following questions to see whether they accord with the ideas and practice advocated in this chapter:

How much did I say in the foreign language during that lesson?

Is there anything I said in English which could easily be said in the foreign language?

How many '*phrases utiles*' and stock formulæ did I use?

In question-and-answer work could I have used the augmented question more frequently and interposed comment or statement?

Was there any situation, activity, mime, or display of visuals where I could have made some remark, comment, or said anything at all in the foreign language?

How much use did I make of explanation, synonym, paraphrase or example in the foreign language?

How much language did the children hear from native sources other than my own voice?

If the answers to the majority of these questions are unsatisfactory, then it is absurd to imagine or expect that the children's ability to understand the foreign language in its spoken form is being fostered and developed.

8

Encouraging Talk between Children

In Chapter 4 we stressed the need for movement and activity on the children's part, the need for them to act out language and not remain as mere passive spectators. Ways were suggested in which two, three, or even small groups of children could be actively involved in varied activities during most phases of the language learning process. Action chains, mime, rôle-playing and all kinds of pursuits where there is some physical movement are vital ingredients in an effective programme of language learning. In this chapter we are concerned not principally with the need for physical movement nor with the oral responses given by children to the teacher's questions; we are concerned with precise techniques and procedures devised to encourage oral interchange between individual children within the class.

In many classes it is the teacher who provides the stimuli to which the class or a single pupil responds. If it is not the teacher providing the stimuli, then it is a tape-recorder in class or laboratory. There is no doubt that in the elementary stages of the language course the teacher must necessarily be the central source of information, the chief guide and pattern-setter. It is not necessary or desirable, however, that he should remain the only questioner, the persistent interrogator in an eternal dialogue between him and the pupils, term after term. It is not easy to relinquish the rôle of questioner, for one needs to know the exact ways and means of doing so. A detailed knowledge of techniques is required.

Putting a number of questions to individuals is basic to good teaching, but there comes a point where pupils must receive opportunities of formulating different types of question. Sometimes they never direct their utterances to anybody other than the teacher. There is often a marked absence of oral exchange between any two children within the class. Techniques need to be developed which allow individuals to address their fellow learners. Throughout any language course every effort should be given to providing progressively more and more scope for pupils to evoke responses from each other.

If oral exchange is always between teacher and pupil, and the teacher's technical repertoire and range of question forms are fairly restricted, then the children will soon become bored with the situation in which they are always at the receiving end and their responses are always dependent on the teacher's stimuli. We use the terms 'stimulus' and 'response' here in order to show that they are not synonymous with 'question' and 'answer' as is sometimes supposed. They are meant to be much broader terms, and it is important that the teacher realises this if he wishes to add to his repertoire of classroom procedures.

A stimulus need not be a question, and a response need not be a direct answer to the question. The teacher can say a sentence in the form of a statement and the pupils can imitate it; this is, in fact, a stimulus-response exercise. It may be that the teacher gives a mother-tongue sentence in spoken form and the pupils give the foreign-language equivalent. Pupils can also be taught to handle various substitution and transformation exercises. An original sentence pattern is provided and three or four pupils are called on to change the subject, verb, object or an adverbial phrase. A series of contradictions and a slight variation in the pattern help to contextualise the following drill, for example:

Teacher: *Jean-Paul arrive à la gare.*
Pupil A: *Mais non, Pierre arrive à la gare.*
Pupil B: *Mais non, c'est Claude qui arrive à la gare.*
Pupil C: *Mais non, je crois que c'est Paul qui arrive à la gare.*

The class needs to become versed in the pattern of the overall framework so that this procedure involving three pupil responses can be used for other sentences and other vocabulary items. In another drill the verb might be changed by each pupil or the destination, and so on.

A stimulus may take the form of a sound on the tape, a gesture, or a picture, or a mime; different pupils give verbal responses to each sound:

C'est un oiseau qui chante.
C'est un chien qui aboie.
C'est un lion qui rugit.

In each case the pattern the response is to take can be predetermined by teacher and class. As soon as practice has been gained with each individual pupil giving the above verbal response to the sound stimulus, the class can progress in a later lesson to the kind of drill where pupil follows pupil within a slightly more flexible, yet strictly controlled, framework:

Stimulus on tape: Sound of dog barking.
Pupil A (contradicts obvious answer): *C'est un oiseau qui chante.*
Pupil B: *Mais non, c'est un chien.*
Pupil C: *Oui, bien sûr, c'est un chien qui aboie.*
Pupil D: *C'est vrai. Tu as raison, Jean.*

In a way each response is also the stimulus for the following utterance; the remark of pupil B is the stimulus for pupil C's remark and so forth. The precise form of each sentence pattern, including word-groups like '*bien sûr*', '*c'est vrai*', '*tu as raison*', is carefully predetermined and practised. The framework is then used for a whole series of sound stimuli.

A stimulus may take the form of a command or a request. When this is the case the response will often be the carrying out of an action not involving any verbal utterance at all. When the class has reached the intermediate or advanced stage of a course and has mastered the imperative forms of a number of action verbs, various pupils can perform the action in the classroom and then choose an instruction for the next pupil to carry out. Several figurines or picture-cards can help in this kind of work since they can be taken and placed on, near, or under different objects about the room; they can also be passed from pupil to pupil. Only one or two of the brighter children will be doing this to begin with, but as the term's work progresses the teacher tries to create a longer chain of actions involving several individuals:

Pupil A (to next selected pupil): *Allez au tableau noir, prenez la craie jaune et dessinez une chaise.*
Pupil B: *Venez à la table, prenez le livre rouge et mettez-le près de la porte, etc.*

A chain of stimulus-response utterances in which the teacher and four or five individual pupils are involved forms the foundation for more adventurous activities such as the acting out of dialogues, the performing of playlets and group work. These drills also lay the foundation for getting the children to produce creative novel sentences.

The kind of activity work in which a pupil issues one or more commands involving the imperative form of verbs to be carried out by another pupil, cannot be undertaken without adequate build-up of practice by gradual steps over a period of some weeks. A useful type of work which can precede it is directed dialogue. Directed dialogue is controlled by the teacher's request to an individual pupil to ask another pupil to say or do something:

Guillaume, dis à Paul de toucher l'oreille droite.
Étienne, demande à Jeanne de dessiner un avion au tableau noir.
Bernard, demande à Vincent s'il a faim.

The pattern here is teacher + pupil + pupil, which may appear easy to operate at first glance. Such a procedure, however, will only be successful when the pupils have mastered the necessary linguistic elements required in their response. It also demands skill and practice on the teacher's part.

We have given examples in this section of the type of work in which the teacher provides a basic sentence and the pupils in turn make various substitutions and transformations. First of all, in the early stages, the pupils will change just the subject or just the verb. Each pupil will follow the pattern by repeating the sentence, but he will offer an alternative linguistic item in a given slot:

À deux heures il est entré dans la maison.
À deux heures il est entré dans le café.
À deux heures il est entré dans l'église, etc.

The pupils continue to change items in a single slot until no more offers are forthcoming from anybody in the class. The teacher then indicates a different slot by providing a model answer and the pupils continue:

À trois heures il est entré dans l'église.
À cinq heures il est entré dans l'église.
À dix heures il est entré dans l'église, etc.

The teacher may call a halt when he wishes. After this single slot substitution has become an established practice with a particular class, a process that may take some months, it will be possible to proceed to random slot replacement where a pupil must change a different part of the sentence from that changed by the previous pupil:

À six heures le facteur est entré dans la maison.
À sept heures *le facteur est entré dans la maison.*
À sept heures le facteur est entré dans le bureau de poste.
À sept heures le facteur est sorti du *bureau de poste.*
À sept heures le vieillard *est sorti du bureau de poste.*

This type of exercise in which four pupils each deal with one slot in a four-slot sentence requires concentration, alertness, a good aural memory and a thoughtful response. The pupil has to listen very carefully to the person answering before him. Incorrect substitutions or unacceptable combinations are to be promptly checked by the teacher. Since it is a more difficult exercise than that in which the same slot is dealt with by the pupils, it must come later in the language programme. It is only at an advanced stage that the class can come to an even more complex exercise described in the next paragraph. They should then be one more step along the path to creating their own sentences from their memory store.

The grading of material and of procedures according to the simplicity or difficulty of the oral response required is essential for successful performance and progress. If the teacher has made frequent use of the techniques and exercises suggested in the previous paragraph and if the class can perform with confidence the manipulations involved in random slot replacement, it is then possible to introduce structural or pattern drills in which two and more elements are changed. This kind of work presupposes that the class have reached a fair standard of oral proficiency and have built up, perhaps over a period of four or five years, a knowledge of verb forms, nouns and adverbial phrases on which they can call. With this stage of creative pattern drills it may be considered helpful to rely on visual support by having the model pattern displayed on the screen:

À dix heures et quart | Jean | est entré dans | le restaurant.

Pupils are then called upon to change elements in two slots only:

À six heures et demie *Jean est entré dans* la gare.
À dix heures et quart Vincent est sorti du *restaurant, etc.*

They then change elements in three slots and finally in all four slots so that the original sentence is completely replaced by a new one which retains the same pattern:

À une heure le facteur est arrivé à la Poste.
À trois heures l'agent est allé à la pharmacie, etc.

Some teachers may consider that this last type of replacement drill is better suited to written work. It may, of course, form the basis of a written homework exercise, and should be used before the pupils reach the stage of free written composition.

Let it not be thought that the pattern drill type of work we have exemplified is the same thing as structural drilling in the language laboratory. Although the same principle of controlling linguistic structure is involved, there are essential points of difference. In the usual language laboratory type of drill the word or phrase to be fitted into any given slot is always provided as a cue on the tape. In the above exercises a good deal of 'creativity' is demanded since the learner has to recall from

63

memory a suitable item to replace one he has just heard. The second point of difference is that the above exercises do not have a confined framework of tape or teacher stimulus plus pupil response. Children cultivate the habit of listening to other children, and at the advanced stages there is more scope for producing 'novel utterances' in a normal classroom situation.

A further form of work preparatory to oral interchange within the class is what can be called quite simply sentence-building. This form of work means not just replacing elements in an original model sentence, but adding bits of language to expand it. Substitution and expansion techniques can function separately at first; later they can be combined. This work consists of incremental drills which allow pupil to follow pupil:

Il mange   *Bernard mange un œuf.*
                     Au café Bernard mange un œuf.

The initial verb form is given and each pupil adds one element; this kind of work moves even further along the path of creativity and novel utterances:

La dame lit.
La dame lit un journal.
La dame lit un journal allemand.
La dame lit un journal allemand dans le train.
La dame lit un journal allemand dans le train de six heures.
Assise en face de son mari, la dame lit un journal allemand dans le train de six heures.

With this kind of exercise intensive individual repetition practice is assured. It can also become an interesting game-like activity demanding good memory powers. The game in which various items are added to a shopping list ('My aunt went to market' may be familiar to many teachers) can be usefully employed in the class:

Je suis allé au marché pour acheter du beurre, du fromage et des pommes.
Je suis allé au marché pour acheter du beurre, du fromage, des pommes et des poires.

Je suis allé au marché pour acheter du beurre, du fromage, des pommes, des poires et des légumes, etc.

This procedure may be used as an effective revision tool:

Dans le jardin zoologique j'ai vu des lions, des tigres, des singes et des ours.

Dans le jardin zoologique j'ai vu des lions, des tigres, des singes, des ours et des loups.

The more advanced the pupils the more specific the vocabulary items being revised, practised or tested:

Dans la forêt on trouve des chênes, des sapins et des hêtres.

Dans la forêt on trouve des chênes, des sapins, des hêtres et des marronniers.

Dans le jardin on trouve une bêche, une brouette, un râteau, une fourche, etc.

Once again it should be a question of adding one element at a time and of proceeding, in small steps, from the simple to the more difficult. With pupils who have studied French for five or six years it should not be impossible to build up a whole context or situation defined in terms of a complex sentence. Using the example where we begin with a lady reading we may eventually arrive at:

Assise en face de son pauvre mari, la jolie dame a commencé à lire un journal allemand et le train de six heures est parti pour Paris.

In order to facilitate oral exercises on sentence-building and in order to operate a more natural conversational exchange between pupils it is necessary to teach children how to formulate and ask different types of question. The pupils themselves should be given ample opportunities for putting questions to the teacher and to fellow pupils. Before continuing our description of sentence-building, which involves both structure and vocabulary drills, we need to examine one or two techniques that allow children to practise types of question. This will enable us to illustrate how question-and-answer work can be integrated with the substitution and sentence-building work already exemplified. It is controlled and guided talk between pupils, talk which allows a high degree of creative response, that eventually leads to the development of conversational ability in the foreign language.

During the elementary stage of any language course it is the teacher who will be putting questions to the class. The children should therefore become thoroughly acquainted with questions from the listening point of view, since they have heard them again and again. The first step in teaching pupils the various types of question is through imitation: a number of pupils are called upon to give individual responses as has been described in Chapter 5. The following types of question will need practice:

1. Statement form with question intonation and inversion
   C'est un lion? Est-ce un lion?
   Il va au cinéma? Va-t-il au cinéma?
2. Statement preceded by '*Est-ce que . . .*'
   Est-ce que c'est un mouton?
   Est-ce qu'il jette le ballon?
3. Questions asking 'Who?' and 'What?'
   Qui est-ce? Qui jette le ballon?
   Qu'est-ce que c'est?
   Que fait-il?
4. Questions asking 'Where?' and 'How?'
   Où est le chien? Où va-t-il?
   Comment va-t-il à Paris?
   Comment t'appelles-tu?
5. Using specific questions
   Combien de fenêtres y a-t-il?
   De quelle couleur est cette porte?
   Quel âge a-t-il?
   Quelle heure est-il?
   Quel jour est-ce?
   Quel temps fait-il?

It will be noticed that the questions asking 'When?' and 'Why?' are not included for use in the initial stages. The reason for this is that in most cases such questions require a more elaborate answer. If put into circulation too early '*Quand?*' and

'*Pourquoi?*' will cause difficulties with the oral response; they will be essential from the viewpoint of comprehension, of course, and they can be brought into productive use by pupils at an appropriate moment later in the programme. Apart from the use of the various forms of '*Quel?*' in the specific questions listed above, it can be a useful tool in a more general way during the early part of any programme for practising vocabulary:

> *Quel fruit aimes-tu?*
> *Quel animal est le plus petit?*
> *Quels meubles y a-t-il dans la chambre?*
> *Quel moyen de transport choisis-tu?*
> *Quelle partie du corps (de la maison, etc.) est-ce?*

Question work needs to be finely graded as suggested towards the end of Chapter 6. Questions involving the third person of the verb are in general easier than those involving the second person, since often they require no switch in pattern between question and answer:

> Qu'est-ce qu'*il mange?*   *Il mange* une banane.

It is suggested, therefore, that the work is graded in such a way that these third person patterns are established before dealing with second and first person patterns.

After the imitation and repetition phases in learning the question forms the bright pupils can give a lead by acting the rôle of teacher, asking questions about a particular visual. To begin with, the pupil will ask questions on a visual about which the teacher has just been asking a number of questions. Later the pupils will not need to rely on a teacher-phase to precede their own efforts. The next step is for the teacher to give practice to individual pupils in the class in asking questions about an initial sentence provided by him:

> Teacher: *Il mange.*
> Pupil A: *Qui mange?*
> Teacher: *Sophie mange.*
> Pupil B: *Qu'est-ce qu'elle mange?*
> Teacher (to class): *Devinez!*

Pupil C: *Est-ce qu'elle mange une banane?*
Teacher: *Non, elle ne mange pas une banane.*
Pupil D: *Est-ce qu'elle mange une pomme?*
Teacher: *Non, elle ne mange pas une pomme, etc.*

Question work becomes a kind of guessing game for the pupils. When the procedural framework has been established over a period of some weeks, a pupil takes over the teacher's part so that conversational exchange begins to operate completely between pupils. The pupil taking the teacher's part can, if required, prepare his final sentence on paper beforehand:

Pupil A: *Il est allé.*
Pupil B: *Qui est allé?*
Pupil A: *Vincent est allé.*
Pupil C: *Où est-il allé?*
Pupil A: *Devinez!*
Pupil D: *Est-il allé au cinéma?*
Pupil A: *Il n'est pas allé au cinéma, etc.*

Guessing should not continue too long and if the class have not guessed the correct answer after five questions pupil A can give it to them.

The next stage in this work is that in which the linguistic elements are invented by the pupils themselves. The teacher or a pupil will be the main questioner, and the other pupils will build up an imaginary situation:

Teacher: *Il joue.*
Pupil A: *Qui joue?*
Pupil B: *Bernard joue.*
Pupil A: *Qu'est-ce qu'il joue?*
Pupil C: *Il joue au tennis.*
Pupil A: *Où est-ce qu'il joue au tennis?*
Pupil D: *Il joue au tennis dans le parc.*

We are now able to return to the discussion of sentence-building, for the example above should make it clear that question-and-answer work is here being employed as a natural means of building a sentence. The types of oral exercise exemplified above cannot function until the intermediate stage when the children have orally mastered each type of question through a number of exercises involving one type of question only. In the initial stage the teacher may merely be naming the colour, for example, of a number of objects he is thinking of so that pupils obtain practice at one specific question:

Teacher: *Je pense à un chien.*
Pupil: *De quelle couleur est-il?*
Teacher: *Il est noir.*

It is only when each type of question has been mastered through a whole range of examples and when simple creative pattern drills and sentence-building drills are familiar to the children, that one can approach more complex combinations where five or six pupils interact. After five years of carefully graded exercises of the type we have described it should not be expecting too much for groups of pupils to engage in conversation, where the group leader has a number of basic verbs as starting points and members of the group methodically expand the sentence through question-and-answer work:

Pupil A (reading from card): *Il a ramassé un objet.*
Pupil B: *Qui a ramassé un objet?*
Pupil C: *Jean-Paul a ramassé un objet.*
Pupil D: *Qu'est-ce qu'il a ramassé?*
Pupil E: *Jean-Paul a ramassé un mouchoir.*
Pupil F: *De quelle couleur est le mouchoir?*

Pupil A: *Le mouchoir est blanc.*
Pupil B: *Jean-Paul a ramassé un mouchoir blanc.*
Pupil C: *Où est-ce qu'il a ramassé le mouchoir blanc?*
Pupil D: *Dans la rue.*
Pupil E: *Jean-Paul a ramassé le mouchoir blanc dans la rue.*
Pupil F: *Dans quelle rue a-t-il ramassé le mouchoir? etc.*

Whenever a pupil gives a shortened answer ('*le mouchoir est blanc*', '*dans la rue*') the game demands that the next pupil states the sentence in full. The essential point is that the children need to be trained in the exact patterning of any procedural framework within which they are to operate. The combinations of patterns are innumerable, but the more complex the pattern the greater is the need to proceed in carefully programmed steps from the simple to the more difficult. With a more complex pattern it may be that the teacher begins with a statement, three pupils repeat the statement in turn, a fourth pupil expands the statement, a fifth pupil asks a question about the added segment, a sixth pupil answers the question and a seventh contradicts the expanded statement by putting it into the negative form. With a great deal of thought, imagination and ingenuity such exercises can be contextualised so that they closely resemble the give and take of natural speech in realistic situations.

If children always have to depend on the teacher to provide the stimulus for every single response they make, and have little opportunity to create segments of language from their own memory store, then learning to speak a foreign language becomes a restricted and dull routine remote from the real-life situation where there is a constant oral exchange with a number of different individuals and a constant inventiveness of production. Language development implies the asking of questions, requesting, demanding, denying, exclaiming, describing, refusing, making comment, and expressing one's feelings, needs and thoughts about somebody or something. It implies the creation of an infinite variety of sentences using a finite number of structures and vocabulary items. To mimic and parrot under continual adult prompts is only the initial part of language learning. The forms of work and procedures advocated in this chapter will help to shift the heavy burden of oral work from the teacher's shoulders to the pupils themselves.

Especially at the intermediate and advanced stages of his total language programme the teacher needs to ask:

Am I trapped in a question-and-answer procedure that involves teacher-pupil, teacher-pupil, teacher-pupil in a continual dialogue?

Am I setting up frameworks which encourage a chain sequence of teacher + pupil + pupil + pupil . . .?

Am I using techniques that allow a number of pupils to ask various types of question?

Are the children using the imperative forms?

Are we making use of exercises involving substitution and sentence-building where the children provide the linguistic items?

Am I grading the forms of work in carefully programmed steps from the simple to the more complex over the whole year's course?

Many of the procedures exemplified in this chapter serve as an introduction to group work, and the teacher can easily apply them in this area where conditions are favourable. The main intention, however, is to examine those procedures and techniques that can ease the sometimes abrupt transition from the teacher-class situation to the group-learning situation. Class lessons in which pupils learn the basic procedures are an essential foundation for successful group work. Even with the necessary preparatory work many less able pupils will be able to participate fully only in some of the more simple procedural frameworks advocated. The teacher needs, therefore, to develop in the first instance the less complex chain sequences where the less able pupils are not put at a disadvantage because of their more limited memory-span and creative abilities.

9

Making Content Interesting and Relevant

Some lessons centre round the teaching of particular constructions and grammar points. Attention is focused often on isolated
words and how they are synthesised into a given construction.
The blackboard may well be covered with individual items like
'*du*', '*aux*', '*venir de*', '*commencer à*', '*trop de*', '*le lui*',
'*donnerait*', '*venues*', '*ne . . . pas*', '*les miennes*', '*cherche la
bague*', and so on.

A great deal of time is sometimes spent explaining formal
features connected with tense, pronoun use, prepositions with
certain verbs, agreement of past participles, use of the subjunc-
tive, etc. In such cases there may be plenty of oral practice with
sentences containing the grammar points or there may be hardly
any oral work, but what is most evident is the absolute concentration on language as language rather than on language as a
medium for conveying meaningful messages. The emphasis is on
form, not content.

Cautious avoidance of the dangers of a grammatical approach
may well lead to an adherence to oral question-and-answer
techniques, but the emphasis on form can still be overplayed.
Since oral teaching has to be concerned initially with the forming
of habits and the acquisition of skills, the lesson often deals
exhaustively with one or two sentence-patterns and little else. The
whole focus of attention is on 'hammering home', through much
repetition, the linguistic pattern or structure in question. What is

72

lacking is a sequence of messages with a meaningful content which attracts the interest of the children.

Whether the teacher's techniques and general approach are 'traditional' or 'progressive' in character, lessons may reveal an absence of topic, of situation, of interesting context. The objectives and the development of the lessons are strongly determined by formal linguistic precepts, and this results in an obvious lack of interesting subject-matter. Mastery of lexical items within a structural pattern takes precedence over any natural communication of informational content or exchange of ideas. The thing which seems to dominate the teacher's modes of behaviour, and consequently the children's outlook, is an urgent and ever-pressing need to cover a particular number of specified grammar points and vocabulary items. Because the teacher is obliged to deal with a given syllabus or course programme, he erroneously concludes that there can be no substantial and meaningful subject-matter and no communication of interesting and relevant facts in which the children take an interest. The formal elements of the foreign language rather than the messages conveyed tend to colour the work of the lesson. This approach in language teaching inevitably lowers the motivation of many children. No learner wants to wait from five to eight years before he uses language as a means to an end, as a vehicle whereby he can acquire some pleasure from listening to, speaking, reading and writing something interesting.

Mastery of the basic structures and vocabulary items is of course essential. The skills of understanding and of speaking are developed through much hard and intensive practice. Language learning implies an ability to analyse sentences into specific linguistic segments and to recombine known segments into new sentences. Oral proficiency presupposes an exquisite capacity to recognise the function and rôle of various segments and their place within the sentence-pattern. The foreign-language lesson is peculiar among the subjects of the curriculum in that the means of communication has to be acquired before it can be used for its proper ends: to deal with other things. All these truths, however, should not mean that language lessons must always remain turned in upon themselves, presenting language as an object for inspection and dissection and nothing more. In the intermediate and advanced stages of the school programme, that is after certain elementary points have been mastered, it is quite possible to use exercises and texts which have some intrinsic interest while still teaching a specific grammar point.

Both course-makers and teachers should make every attempt to examine content as well as structure. The relevance of what is being said and why it is being said must be carefully pondered. Many courses built along structural lines fail to give due weight to relevance and interest of the subject-matter. Each event, situation, action and topic needs to be carefully selected for its intrinsic merit and its relevance to the natural interests and curiosity of the age-group being taught. Even sentences which embody a particular grammar point can form a meaningful sequence if carefully selected and ordered. If the teacher is anxious to give practice in the perfect tense of reflexive verbs, for example, he may group sentences so that they have a situational context. A sequence of visuals will help towards this contextualisation:

> *Le matin, le forçat s'est réveillé à quatre heures.*
> *Il voulait gagner la frontière avant l'aurore.*
> *Sans hésiter, il s'est levé.*
> *Puis il s'est lavé brusquement dans le ruisseau.*
> *Il ne s'est pas rasé parce qu'il avait perdu son rasoir dans la lutte.*
> *Ensuite il a ramassé sa chemise râpée et s'est habillé.*
> *Il entendait déjà les cris des soldats.*

Additional phrases indicating time, place or reason are essential instruments for ensuing question-and-answer work:

> *À quelle heure est-ce qu'il s'est réveillé?*
> *Où est-ce qu'il s'est lavé?*
> *Pourquoi ne s'est-il pas rasé?*

The demands of structural progression and the demands of situational context are not incompatible, but a great deal of knowledge and skill is required to strike a balance between the two. A good course will strike a nice balance.

Acquiring interesting factual knowledge while practising a certain construction is not impossible. For example, if the teacher is anxious for the children to master the superlative of adjectives and adverbs, the sentences used can give information on the tallest building in the world, the largest town, the longest river, the oldest person, the fastest animal, and so on. The comparative allows even wider scope: is one town larger than another, is this animal faster than that, is steel heavier than lead, do camels live longer than monkeys, is gold harder than silver, is $5°$ centigrade colder than $25°$ fahrenheit? When this principle of informational content is examined and extended one may see that it touches upon a large part of many other aspects and subjects in the school curriculum. It also bears directly on the teaching of 'civilisation' aspects of the culture and country whose language is being learnt. For the purposes of our discussion we shall deal with the 'civilisation' aspects separately from the link with other areas of the curriculum.

The content of sentences practised in class, of textual material, of the visual aids themselves and of the activities undertaken, can with forethought relate to other areas of the curriculum. If this is done children are more likely to acquire an awareness that language is a vehicle of communication relevant to all activities encountered in their school day. It is all very well to state as a main principle that language is a medium for conveying messages, but such a statement needs to be translated into practical terms. If the sentences used in class have a high degree of informational content as illustrated in the previous paragraph, then the principle will be immediately obvious to the children.

There are many situations and topics which provide a basis for a wide range of arithmetical calculations. The routine of assessing the number of boys and girls present at registration, the number taking school meals and other such matters provides an occasion for the teacher to count in French in a realistic and natural way. When teaching time by the clock it is possible to use a number of questions involving simple calculations:

Combien de minutes y a-t-il dans une heure?
Combien de minutes y a-t-il dans un quart d'heure?

Combien de quarts d'heure est-ce qu'il y a dans trois heures?
Il y a combien de secondes dans cinq minutes? etc.

Dealing with the day's date offers an occasion for asking how many days in a certain month, how many days in a week, how many months in a year, and so on.

At a more advanced stage of the course the teacher can ask what the date was five days ago, last Saturday, and so on. The height and weight of pupils, the height of well-known buildings and constructions, the distances between towns, countries, and how long journeys take by foot, by bicycle, by train can help to teach French measurements. Money transactions in shopping scenes help children to handle the foreign coinage with ease, and involve them again in weights and measures. Competitive runners and swimmers in the class can be asked to submit their best times for various distances and different strokes. Pupils can be asked how long a football or netball game lasts, how high they can jump, etc. Simple calculations of adding together mentally two and three numbers, of subtracting and easy multiplication can form the basis of individual and team games where points are given to the first pupil giving the correct answer. Geometric figures and pattern work can provide visual contexts for addition, subtraction, multiplication and division, and for learning fractional parts; coloured circles and squares can be built up into graphs showing how many pupils walk to school, how many cycle, how many come by bus, and so on.

The links with the sciences and with geography are made evident to the children when dealing with map work, the weather, temperature, heat and light, animal and plant life, organs of the body, locomotion and so on. Question-and-answer work on a map of France or Europe can embrace simple factual information while practising basic sentence-patterns and vocabulary: What is the capital of France? Which is the second largest town? What is the name of this river? Is this mountain range the Pyrenees? Is it further from Dieppe to Marseilles than it is from Dieppe to Berlin? Which is the smaller town? Which countries border on France? What is the main industry of this region? What are the main products of that region? Can you name two coastal towns in this area? Is France twice as big as England or four times as big?

At an advanced level more information on current affairs on the European scene can grow out of this basic map work. Once the names of animals and plants have been acquired lesson material can proceed to matters such as how the otter lives, what a bat feeds on, what the natural habitat of the deer is, what countries the cactus is found in, which flowers like damp soil and are found near the river, what tree this shape leaf comes from, which animals hibernate, how you look after a tortoise, which animals provide furs, and so on.

At Sixth Form level good use can be made of elementary textbooks on biology, chemistry, physics, botany, zoology, geography and geology intended for French schools. There is no reason why the languages section of the school library should be restricted to books on French literature and to fiction. The organs of the body can be related to their specific functions, parts of the car can lead to how it works and involve simple mechanics, electricity, heat transmission and other aspects of physics. All these topics can be treated as the basis for graded question-and-answer oral work, first at the intermediate then at the advanced stages of the language teaching programme.

The links with physical education are particularly relevant to the principle of involving children in movement and activity as tentatively expounded in Chapter 4. Any avenues which can link a foreign language with physical education and games should be thoroughly explored. In the First and Middle schools it may well be that there exist teachers who are able to take a given class or group for these activities and integrate them with the foreign language. Much depends on the organisation of the school and the structuring of the curriculum. Physical education offers good opportunities for developing children's aural comprehension and, just as important, for getting them to react in a natural manner to instructions, commands and requests put in the foreign language: '*Jean, va chercher les deux ballons rouges*', '*courez vite au mur*', '*jette la balle à Victor*', '*sautez dix fois comme ça*', '*couche-toi sur le dos*', '*tournez le corps à droite, à gauche*', '*restez sur place*', '*rangez-vous au fond*', etc. The language involved embraces not just the affirmative and negative form of verb imperatives but also adverbs, nouns, prepositions and adjectives. In a game of netball, football and other athletic activities teacher-talk is freed from the restrictions of the normal classroom situation and a good deal can be done by the teacher who is orally fluent in the foreign language.

Dance, movement and drama offer similar opportunities for teacher-talk in the foreign language. In Chapter 4 we touched on the possibilities of mime through game-like activity and question-and-answer work. Miming the actions of different domestic and wild animals can embrace commands from the teacher and guessing by the children. Dialogues and playlets, especially when they involve dressing up and using a range of props and materials, can help to meet the requirement of active exploitation and realistic use of language and the necessity to forge bonds between language, concepts and the real objects and situations to which they refer. Every object is a visual aid for contextualising language.

Art and craft are areas of the curriculum where various materials can aid the process of relating the foreign language to real objects and purposeful activities. The teacher who is orally competent can refer to the fabrics, the paintings, the objects in the paintings, parts of models, the process of putting things together, making objects, adding to things in progress, and in general he can use the foreign language in the concrete ways suggested in Chapter 7.

Cookery, needlework and home economics are often areas in the curriculum where there is a setting and atmosphere that give scope for talk in the foreign language; operations are preceded by instructions which can include at least some incidental and subsidiary statements in the foreign language, while still retaining English for the clarity of essential advice. While the children are then actually engaged in performing varied operations teacher-talk can, when appropriate, relate directly to the children's actions.

Links with music and song are evident in many existing courses: popular songs, folk songs, hymns and carols can be performed with zest and enjoyment, adding a new and stimulating dimension to the language programmes which are carefully structured and contain much hard drill-like forms of work. When linked with drama, instrumental accompaniment using recorders and the musical talents of individuals can help to engage a number of pupils in active participation. In such broader schemes the actual segments of language used and the exact ways in which they relate to the musical activity undertaken have to be carefully analysed. Control of structure and vocabulary and the need for programmed steps and graded material still remain central to the language learning process, and these matters need to be worked out in detail whenever any integrated schemes are attempted.

It is obvious from what we have been suggesting that many difficulties lie in the way of integrating different areas of the curriculum with a view to using the foreign language at times and places other than those specifically intended for set lessons. It is obvious also from our examination of other subject areas that barriers need to be broken down: the content and materials relating to other subjects need incorporating into the language lessons while at the same time language teaching techniques need extending outwards to the other lessons. In the First and Middle schools this ideal is a laudable one and in many small ways its implementation is feasible. In the Secondary schools and High schools difficulties seem insurmountable, but our remarks on the principle of informational content and on mathematics, science and geography are certainly both valid and relevant to the present situation.

Co-operation and purposeful discussion between staff are essential, and the need for staff who are orally proficient in the foreign language is self-evident. To attain some kind of integration between French and other subjects, it is clearly necessary to get discussions going and co-operation amongst the various members of staff. In any given situation it is probable that one or two subject specialists will be more open to this kind of co-operation than others, and obviously it is best to start with them. Broader educational aspects and organisational issues affecting the whole school are naturally fundamental to the problem of using the foreign language as a natural vehicle for communication. And we are still in the position of having to inculcate basic skills before the principle can be effectively put into practice wholeheartedly. What is clear, however, is that the present 'compartmentalised' nature of the foreign-language lesson does not help us or the children to regard language as a means to an end, as a natural vehicle for conveying messages.

Lessons which centre on the teaching of particular constructions and grammar points and have little regard for content at any level of the total programme, only serve to enhance compartmentalisation and make the foreign-language lessons even more restrictive than they need to be. To teach language as though it were an end in itself, and not a means of referring to the myriad facets of the world we live in, is a cardinal error of language teaching.

Apart from developing in children an awareness that the foreign language can be related to all activities and experiences encountered in their school day, the principle of informational content has a further, more specific, implication: the need to teach about the general culture and 'civilisation' of the people whose language is being learned. This embraces much more than the history and literary highlights of the foreign 'civilisation' and, although often considered most relevant to the advanced stages of the course, has fairly wide application at all levels of the programme.

Even at the most elementary stage, pupils need to realise that the use of simple everyday words in the foreign language often involves new and different concepts rooted in the foreign culture. '*Pain*', '*vin*', '*boîte aux lettres*', '*cave*', '*agent*' mean something different in the French context from their English equivalents in their English context. The distinctive connotations of the French words are best acquired when they are directly associated with authentic visuals portraying the foreign culture. Taken in its widest sense the new 'culture' will always be inherent in every bit of language we teach.

We have already shown how geographical aspects of the country whose language is being studied can form the substance of lessons. Through the use of maps, slides, filmstrips, transparencies with overlays and sound films much factual information about the country, its products and its industries, its life and its customs, can be presented in audio-visual form and can provide fodder for question-and-answer work and many other exercises and activities. Distinctive features of the foreign culture will be presented via the visual and the textual materials used in class.

Without the use of both non-projected and projected material the children would never gain entry to all these features typical of the French way of life, the very things which make the language more meaningful. Children have a natural interest in how ordinary French people live, their hobbies, pastimes, the games they play, what they eat and drink, what jobs they do, what kind of bicycles and cars they have, what their houses are like, what they do at Christmas, what French children do at school, what clothes they wear, and so on. Children's interest in these aspects, however, soon dies if it is not stimulated through good authentic visual materials. These visual materials can range from comic drawings, through photographs and slides, to sound films. The important point is that these patterns of life and daily routines of the French people and the information concerning them need to issue naturally out of the main course and forms of work.

Children need to learn about the working of the telephone, the buying of bus tickets, the way the *Métro* works, French post-boxes, the '*code de la route*', policemen, meal-times, the nature of the '*café*' and the cinema, railways, markets, circuses, '*la loterie nationale*' '*jours de fête*', and all those features that give the French way of life its distinctive flavour. Any good course will reveal these various facets in context and express them in language readily understood by children. Integration of language and content can only be effected if considerable thought is given to the control of sentence-patterns and vocabulary items in the foreign language. Knowledge of the features we have listed should develop subtly over a period of time as they arise naturally out of the linguistic progression of the programme.

Although we are here principally concerned with the language as a vehicle for conveying information on various aspects of 'civilisation', it must be mentioned that there is a case for dealing with these aspects in English where classes of less able children have continually experienced failure in acquiring the basic language skills. Sometimes such an approach can rescue classes and help to motivate them. It is once again a question of balance. The teacher, if dealing with such topics in English, can always introduce a minimum number of expressions and words in the foreign language related to what he is talking about. Such short phrases and word-groups can form the nucleus of sentences for language study. The teacher can subtly build around short units like '*Il a gagné la loterie nationale*', '*Il est sorti du cinéma à une heure*', or '*Il y a un terrain de camping dans le Bois de Boulogne*', while using English as the main vehicle for discussion about France.

Whatever the teacher's attitude towards such an approach, he should never underestimate the ability of less able children to extract information from material presented in the foreign language when they are motivated to do so. The development of aural comprehension is a worthwhile pursuit with less able children provided the content is something they are interested in.

At the intermediate stage of the language course acquaintance with the features we have mentioned will lead on to a study of broader aspects such as those which embrace the process of making wine from grapes; technical achievements associated with hydro-electric dams, air-liners, cars; achievements in architecture, roads, industry; French tapestries, cookery, regional costumes and customs; various occupations; information on national and local government; aspects of social and religious institutions; educational establishments and how they work; radio and television programmes; magazines and journals; and so on. At the advanced stage pupils will lead on to the study of various regions of France; its history and principal scientists, painters, musicians, authors and politicians; its political, commercial, industrial activities; the press and publishing; and so on. In the Sixth Form texts chosen for study need not be restricted to those of a literary nature. Passages can be culled from contemporary newspapers and journals, and can embrace current affairs, banking and economics, the law and politics, news items, sporting events, advertising, engineering and technology, psychology and the sciences, and so on.

If there is a gradual mastery of the basic skills of oral fluency and reading ability and a growing command of sentence-patterns and vocabulary during the first few years of learning the foreign language, there should be an ever-increasing opportunity to shift the emphasis from the form of the language to the content. What is being said will always be contending with how something is said for the central position on the stage throughout the whole course programme. The value of the messages being conveyed must be continually inspected and judged, otherwise language teaching lapses into the formal, the trivial and the superficial. Language becomes a skeleton with no body, no flesh and no life.

The following questions will help the teacher to attend to the matters we have been discussing and guide him away from teaching about the foreign language towards teaching something in the foreign language:

Am I always concentrating in my lessons on grammar points?

Do I ever consider the subject-matter, the content, the 'message' and meaning of the sentences being practised?

Can I convey some interesting fact or observation in the sentences being practised?

In what specific ways can I emphasise much more the topic, the situational aspects of the work I am doing?

Can I give a contextual sequence in a realistic setting to the examples we are practising in class?

Can I relate these particular grammar points and vocabulary items to any of the other areas of the curriculum to give them relevance?

Is the content of these visuals, this text and these forms of exercise interesting, informative and useful?

Am I teaching the children something about the country and the life of the people whose language they are learning?

10

Achieving Continuity and Defining Objectives

There need to be clear differences between materials and techniques used with a class of ten-year-olds and those used with a class of fourteen-year-olds. Well-tried techniques may well be basic to both, but what needs to be examined are the specific differences which we might expect with regard to those features that mark the development, continuity and progression of linguistic performance. How do we recognise and achieve an ever-growing competence in mastery of the basic skills from one point to another in any language teaching programme?

In some cases the amount of language presented to the children and handled by them remains the same in the class of younger children as some years later. The grammar points and examples being practised may show no increase in complexity and are sometimes the very same points. With audio-visual and oral techniques there may be no extension of repertory or forms of work. In the fourteen-year-old class of pupils who have learned French for four or more years the length of utterances and the speed of oral response may be no different from that observed in the class of ten-year-olds. A greater wealth of vocabulary is not always apparent, the structures are no more complex, creative responses are not more numerous, errors are not less frequent. Indeed, in some cases, motivation may be lower with the class of older children, and less interest and more apathy might be more rampant.

We cannot expect firm progress, an increased mastery of the

skills, unless specific techniques are developed to meet the growing needs of the pupils at each stage of the total programme. Many reasons are put forward for the absence of continual growth and development in the language skills from year to year in the school programme, an absence which, we must stress, is not peculiar to foreign-language teaching. Some reasons are very general and point to fundamental changes in the emotional attitudes of the children. Other reasons are more tangible yet nonetheless intractable. One of these points to the inevitable problem of staff changes which always act as a brake on any developmental progress over a period of years. How often do we hear the complaint that a particular class have learned next to nothing because Mr X or Miss Y took them the previous year: 'She was hopeless; she's left now of course. I've tried to start from scratch more or less'! The remark is unprofessional but frank, and the best scapegoats are absent ones.

Not only do staff changes affect continuity and build-up of techniques, more and more complex forms of work and modes of operation within a school, but also a lack of a common approach among members of the language department can have a similar influence. For successful progression from year to year there must be close collaboration between the language staff. They must work as a team with common techniques and common objectives, knowing how each other operates in the classroom. Since teachers are often very individual and independent beings seeking personal salvation within their own classrooms, however, it is not always easy to achieve the desired collaboration. Much depends on the leadership qualities of the Head of the Languages Department.

Other reasons for absence of continuity, progression and development from one year to the next with a given group of pupils may be found in poor planning and in limited techniques. A course programme or basic syllabus needs to be seen in its entirety from beginning to end, however flexible or schematic it might be. However great the practical difficulties already mentioned, it is still essential to define broad objectives for each year of the total programme. The types of exercise and forms of work and activities undertaken at each stage should reflect a progressive movement from the simple to the more complex. Teaching techniques and specific classroom procedures should grow in number and become more subtle in their application as we move from stage to stage. Language already learned has to be exploited continually as a basis on which to build and expand.

When we come to examine the language teaching in the upper reaches of a school, in Fifth and Sixth Forms of Secondary schools for example, we find many of the shortcomings outlined in the preceding pages increase fourfold. Instead of the teacher's repertoire of techniques and procedures becoming more abundant, extensive and subtle, it becomes limited, stultified and restricting. Instead of finding teacher and pupils discussing a range of varied texts of different styles and registers, and engaged in varied forms of work and activities, we find them laboriously translating into awkward English pages and pages of some sophisticated literary text or ploughing through arid drills and written exercises in an attempt to grasp grammatical complexities and fine shades of meaning not always fully appreciated by French speakers themselves. Instead of finding all talk in the foreign language we find a preponderance of English. Instead of finding a greater use of language laboratory equipment, slides and sound films we meet an attitude that considers them irrelevant, extraneous and time-wasting. Oral interaction between pupils and involvement with the 'civilisation' of the country are relegated to a secondary place. Pace slows considerably, varied diet becomes unnecessary, responsibility for consolidating work is passed to the pupils, and the lecture-type lesson takes over.

Many classes in the middle and upper ranges of the Secondary school use course materials intended for earlier years: a Second Year class using a first-year textbook which contains sentence-patterns and vocabulary appropriate to nine or ten-year-old pupils and which contains rather naïve subject-matter, a Fourth Year class of fourteen and fifteen-year-olds using Book Two of a four-book course to G.C.E. or C.S.E. examinations, a Fifth Year class frantically practising constructions and vocabulary items which should have been well established two or three years earlier. At last pupils have become conscious of public examinations and their motivation is often enhanced in their last year of study; naturally the teacher exploits this heightened awareness and this sometimes means cramming the best part of five years work into a single year.

The use of an easier textbook or stage of a course than is appropriate to a particular year may well be justified by the teacher: this material is what the pupils can handle; anything more difficult would only impede progress. The subject-matter, however, will inevitably be too far below that required for the natural interests of the age-group being catered for. Where there may be books in use at the appropriate level (Book Two in a Second Year class and Book Four in the Fourth Year class) it is hardly ever the case that the course books previous to any one of them have been thoroughly mastered by the children. No course ever satisfies the requirements of every teacher or group of pupils, but a good course can at least provide some means of structuring the syllabus, defining what ground is to be covered and measuring the children's progress. Language courses, whether they be of a traditional textbook type or audio-visual in nature, always seem to come in for a great deal of criticism from teachers. Critical comment reveals a healthy spirit, but too often it is the course that is blamed for every language teaching evil under the sun: 'The children find it boring. The visuals are childish. The tapes are terrible. The exercises are too difficult. The texts are dull.' Sometimes the teacher shows his contempt for the course by not using it, preferring instead to rely on his own talents and material: 'Yes, we're supposed to be following it, but I just select bits and pieces. It needs a lot of modifying and adapting, and we also have to supplement it with this, that, and the other.'

If a teacher does not have to rely on a basic course, if his own forms of work and personal material are more suitable and effective, and if he has a clear conception of his total programme and the objectives he wishes to achieve, then all is well and good. This state of affairs, however, is a rare phenomenon, and even the most gifted teachers are members of a team. A programme needs to be planned and objectives need to be defined not just for the year but for several years. If a new teacher is to build on the work of the teacher who taught the class the previous year, then he must know what has been covered. There must be some specification of sentence-patterns, vocabulary, and topic areas covered if the new teacher is to help the children build effectively on what they have already gained. Absence of continuity and progressive development of language mastery from year to year is most marked in those schools where there is no basic set of course materials extending over a number of years, no common methods and objectives among members of the language team and no awareness of the fact that language learning is a cumulative affair.

Apart from the use of inappropriate textbooks at various levels in the school, there is sometimes a tendency to adopt exclusive approaches which swing from audio-visual and oral work on the one hand to reading, writing and translation work on the other hand. Disappointment with the one approach sends the teacher scuttling to the other extreme, without ever being able to realise the nice balance between the skills required at all stages of the total programme.

Instead of observing throughout a programme evidence of any specification of which skills are to receive emphasis at various stages, we find a Second Year class overburdened with written work for which they are not ready and a Fifth Year class engaged in rather elementary audio-visual and question-and-answer work. A sequence in which the emphasis shifts from listening to speaking, from speaking to reading and from reading to writing is difficult to detect. The interrelationship between these four basic skills is badly understood by some teachers, for at one point they are working from the spoken forms to written forms and at another point they are working from written forms to spoken forms. What is more, rules pertaining to the written language are found to form the basis of what are supposed to be exclusively audio-lingual or audio-visual forms of work, whereas it is clear that a descriptive analysis of speech does not correspond to the descriptive analysis of written forms.

The Head of Department in collaboration with his team of language teachers should define in fairly clear terms the objectives and goals for each year's work. Each year's work needs in turn to be related to the total programme for five years or whatever the duration of the children's complete school studies in a given foreign language. Only by viewing the whole can we fully appreciate the function and purpose of the parts. For each year it is possible to specify the linguistic content in terms of grammar points, constructions, idioms and vocabulary items to be mastered by the children. However, this mapping out of a syllabus of language to be taught is not enough. The team should also be concerned with aspects of method, technique, forms of work, audio and visual materials, and with the basic skills and activities that are to receive emphasis. This does not mean a rigidly specified programme; planning can always provide enough scope, freedom and flexibility for the individual teacher to display his own distinctive talents and strengths. The important point is that careful planning and definition of precise objectives at each stage and level can help considerably towards achieving continuity, development, growth and progression.

The overall school programme should concern itself with how much weight is to be given, each term and each year, to the various basic skills: listening, speaking, reading and writing. It may well be that, although there could be a balance of these skills in certain lessons, one particular year will place considerable emphasis on one skill. Perhaps in the first term or so the stress will be on listening practice. Certainly in the first year of learning the foreign language children will not be spending the larger part of every lesson in reading and writing. In the second year it may well be that oral work and speaking practice will receive the main stress. The amount of time given to the development of reading and acquisition of structure and vocabulary by means of reading will be heavy in the middle school classes. In the Fourth and Fifth Years more and more written work might be undertaken. During the Fourth Year writing will be more tightly controlled by question-and-answer work and appropriate exercises, whereas in the Fifth Year there will be more opportunities for composition work and more open-ended exercises.

The emphasis on the various skills will not only differ from year to year but from class to class according to the abilities and attainment of the pupils. It may well be that with slower learners emphasis on listening and speaking skills will be prolonged over a number of years while writing figures little in the programme. The balance between the acquisition of passive vocabulary and actual oral production will need examining at each stage with classes of varying levels of attainment. The balance between visual and textual presentation will also need special attention when oral work is combined with reading.

At various stages and levels within the total programme the rôle and function of visual material will be changing. Visuals will be very closely tied to the linguistic items being taught in the first two years or so, but in the middle school classes the visuals will relate perhaps to longer stretches of reading text. In the Fourth and Fifth Year classes visuals will be of a more generalised nature serving as starting points for written work; it will no longer be necessary to illustrate every sentence used in the lesson. All the various ways in which visuals are used at each stage of the total programme should be discussed at meetings where the members of the language teaching team come together, and in these discussions one should try to be as specific as possible with regard to actual teaching procedure.

The level of oral work expected during each year should reflect a marked cumulation in complexity of structures, in length of utterances, in number of idioms, in speed of delivery, in wealth of vocabulary and in creativity of responses. Each year should witness a building upon the stretches of language already acquired, an expansion and development of actual sentences already mastered, a growing facility for manipulating memorised segments into a greater number of new sentences, and an increasing emphasis on informational content and subject-matter. All forms of work, exercises and drills need to be graded in the manner advocated and illustrated in Chapter 8 so that the children are led by gradual steps towards a mastery of heard and spoken language.

Only through careful overall planning can teachers clearly see the ends to which they are working and the exact means whereby they are setting out to achieve those ends. There must be long-term aims and short-term aims. The short-term achievements can sometimes be justified as ends in themselves, so long as they are appropriate to the age, abilities and aptitude of the group of children in question. The principle of progression, however, needs to find application whether the course be long or short. Members of the Languages Department need to be constantly exchanging ideas not only between themselves and with members of other departments, but with their language colleagues from the Primary or the Middle schools. Where the majority of contributory schools do follow a common course, liaison between schools is vital in exploiting and building on what has already been learned. Continuity of method and materials needs close review.

The following questions will need to be studied and answered:

Does the grammar and vocabulary specified at each stage show a progression from the simple to the complex?

Are there increasing levels of difficulty in the work involving listening comprehension and oral fluency?

Is there an obvious progression in the visual, audio and textual materials used at each stage?

How does the balance of skills change in each year?

What sort of gradation is evident in the forms of work, exercises and drills from year to year?

If such questions and their implications are not examined and discussed, and if there exists no clear definition of aims and objectives, the teacher's work will lack drive and purpose and some teachers may well find themselves treading the same piece of ground no matter what particular year or class they are teaching.

In planning continuity and progression from year to year, and in defining the objectives at each stage in terms of which skills, activities and forms of work are to be emphasised, we need to apply the two basic principles of 'gradation' and 'proportion'. Gradation means breaking up material in steps which are then sequenced from the easy to the more complex and difficult along the lines suggested in Chapter 6 with question work. Proportion refers to the relative amount of lesson time given to presenting structures or vocabulary items, to the practising of the listening, speaking, reading or writing skill, and to using different procedures as exemplified in Chapter 3.

Language learning is essentially a cumulative affair: it begins as a small compact snowball made firm by constant effort, but as it rolls along it gathers speed. With more and more snow quickly and easily attaching itself, the snowball becomes a huge mass. Until we achieve this kind of quickening of pace, this kind of progression and cumulation, so that it characterises the total programme of language teaching throughout a school, we shall never get our pupils to attain that high standard of listening comprehension and oral fluency we so fervently desire. The realisation of this desired goal will never come about unless every language teacher strives to achieve the highest degree of expertise and technical competence as a craftsman.

A Framework of Analysis

As a conclusion and summary of the main techniques and procedures discussed in the ten chapters of this book the following framework of analysis is offered. It is hoped that it may serve as a useful checklist for students, supervisors and others in providing guidance on assessing and improving classroom performance.

The theme of each chapter is brought into sharp focus by showing the negative side of the coin. Each heading refers to the cardinal error which has been reviewed in that chapter. The concepts listed succinctly under each heading are the main ones considered in the text, and many of them lose a good deal of significance if viewed outside the context of what has been said in the text.

1. *Too much talking on the part of the teacher and too little on the part of the children*
(a) Amount spoken in the foreign language by the class
(b) Number of children giving oral responses
(c) Number of children not speaking anything
(d) How carefully are children's responses dealt with

2. *No use of audio or visual aids by teacher or by children*
(a) Use made of tape-recorder
(b) How language laboratory is employed
(c) Use of projected visuals
    Overhead projector
    Slides or filmstrips
    Cineloops or films

(d) Manipulation of non-projected visuals
   Objects
   Pictures and figurines
(e) Exploiting situations within the classroom
(f) Use of mime, actions and dramatisation
(g) Number of children manipulating visual materials

3. *Failure to provide a varied diet*
(a) Different types of activity
(b) Variety of materials and audio-visual aids
(c) Division of lesson into varied types of work
(d) Number of techniques and procedures used
(e) Time devoted to
   Listening   Speaking   Reading   Writing
(f) How much sentence manipulation, exploitation and creation by the children
(g) Amount of varied material from previous lessons

4. *No activity or participation on the part of the children*
(a) Amount of activity work from pupils
(b) Number of pupils performing out of their seat
(c) Children employed in demonstrating teaching points
(d) Children helping in question work
(e) How much rôle-playing and acting out of language
(f) Personal involvement of pupils with lesson materials

5. *Lack of consolidation through repetition and intensive practice with regard to individual children*
(a) Number of times same question asked
(b) Number of individuals allowed to answer same question
(c) How much insistence on higher standards of oral response
(d) How many pupils not responding surely and confidently
(e) How many pupil-language contacts in a lesson

6. *Lack of vigour and pace*
(a) Speed of pupil response in imitation work
(b) Fluency and pace in question work
(c) Correct grading and sequencing of questions

(d) How much emphasis on sentence meanings

7. *Starvation of exposure to a large amount of spoken language*
(a) Amount spoken in the foreign language by the teacher
(b) Use of language with visuals, actions and situations
(c) How much use made in the foreign language of:

'Phrases utiles'	Stock formulæ and clichés
Comment	Statement
Explanations	Paraphrase
Synonym and antonym	Examples of usage
Description and definition	

(d) Authentic speech heard from tape-recorder
    Male voices   Female voices   Children's voices

8. *Lack of oral interaction between children*
(a) Number of pupils addressing other pupils
(b) How many pupil responses in chain sequence
(c) Number of foreign language questions put by pupils
(d) Use of commands formulated by the children
(e) Creative substitution and sentence building by children
(f) Group interaction within the class

9. *Failure to provide interesting content relating to other areas of the curriculum*
(a) How interesting is the subject-matter of the language being practised
(b) What degree of informational content is being conveyed
(c) How much stress on the foreign culture and customs
(d) How much emphasis on topic and situational context
(e) What links are being forged with geography, science and other subjects on the curriculum

10. *Absence of continuity and progression with no clear definition of emphases at each stage of a course*
(a) Linguistic objectives of:

Lesson	Week's work
Term's work	Year's work

(b) Progression over the year with regard to:

Procedures	Forms of work
Wealth of vocabulary	Creative responses
Complexity of structure	Length of utterance
Listening comprehension	Oral fluency

(c) Appropriate level and gradation of material:

    Oral   Textual   Visual

(d) Progression of emphasis from one skill to another over the term and from year to year:

    Listening   Speaking   Reading   Writing

It is impossible to quantify or measure in any precise way a task involving such a complexity of variable factors. Caution is needed, therefore, in any practical application of the framework to analyse and check teacher performance. It would be unwise to draw too many conclusions if using the checklist to assess just two or three lessons in isolation. The analysis covers far more features than could be readily apparent in a few lessons only. Personality characteristics, human relationships, class discipline, children's attitudes, and a host of vital factors must inevitably lie outside the scope of this framework which stresses method and procedure. However, as a means of continuous assessment of the teacher's basic techniques, over a period of time with different classes at various levels, it can provide a useful objective profile of strengths and weaknesses.

Language teaching is an 'art' rather than a 'science'. It is an art requiring a dedicated talent and a missionary zeal, but a large part of the job will always remain a matter of skilled craftsmanship developed with knowledge and training.

Bibliography

This is divided into four separate lists covering the main areas relevant to matters dealt with in this text. I have selected only those texts considered essential to a serious study of language teaching method and those that offer information and practical help to the classroom teacher. The lists should offer sufficient fare for both the teacher in training and the experienced practitioner who wishes to further his own knowledge of modern techniques. Where chapters of these basic books are relevant to aspects dealt with in this text I have merely referred to the author's surname in the notes to each chapter. If the author has written more than one work the date of publication is added to distinguish between them.

The chapter notes contain where it seems particularly relevant details of other useful books of a more general kind and reference to specific language teaching catalogues and materials which exemplify and support suggestions made in the book. These notes are not meant in any way to be exhaustive; they are intended to set the reader on the path for his own researches.

For those who wish to delve more deeply into the linguistics, psychology and pedagogy in relation to language teaching there are three extensive bibliographies worth examining: CENTRE FOR INFORMATION ON LANGUAGE TEACHING AND RESEARCH and the ENGLISH TEACHING INFORMATION CENTRE, *A language-teaching bibliography* (annotated), Cambridge University Press, 2nd edn. 1972; ROBINSON, J. O. *An annotated bibliography of modern language teaching: books and articles* 1946–67, Oxford University Press, 1969; the American ACTFL *Annual bibliography,* for

97

details of which see the journal *Foreign language annals*, Vol. 4, no. 4, May 1971, p. 429, published by the American Council on the Teaching of Foreign Languages, 62 Fifth Avenue, New York, N.Y. 10011. MACKEY's book also contains a lengthy end bibliography.

1. General

BENNETT, W. A. *Aspects of language and language teaching* Cambridge University Press 1968

BILLOWS, F. L. *The techniques of language teaching* Longman 1961

BROOKS, N. *Language and language learning: theory and practice* Harcourt, Brace and World 2nd edn, 1964

COLE, L. R. *Teaching French to juniors* University of London Press, 2nd edn revised and expanded, 1969

CORDER, S. P. *The visual element in language teaching* Longman 1966

CORNELIUS, E. T. *How to learn a foreign language* Crowell Co., New York 1955

DODSON, C. J. *Language teaching and the bilingual method* Pitman 1967

DUTTON, B., ed. *Guide to modern language teaching methods* AVLA Publication No. 1, Cassell 1965

FINOCCHIARO, M. *Teaching children foreign languages.* McGraw-Hill 1964

GOUIN, F. *The art of teaching and studying languages* (translated by H. Swan and V. Bétis) G. Philip 1892

GURREY, P. *Teaching English as a foreign language* Longman 1955

HARDING, D. *The new pattern of language teaching* Longman 1967

HILL, L. A. *Selected articles on teaching English as a foreign language* Oxford University Press 1967

HODGSON, F. M. *Learning modern languages* Kegan Paul 1955

HUEBENER, T. *How to teach foreign languages effectively* New York University Press and University of London Press 1965

HUEBENER, T. *Audio-visual techniques in teaching foreign languages* rev. ed, New York University Press and University of London Press 1967

JESPERSEN, O. *How to teach a foreign language* Allen and Unwin 1904. Reprinted 1956

LADO, R. *Language teaching: a scientific approach* McGraw-Hill 1964

LIBBISH, B., ed. *Advances in the teaching of modern languages, vol. 1* Pergamon 1963

MACKEY, W. F. *Language teaching analysis* Longman 1965

MALLINSON, V. *Teaching a modern language* Heinemann 1953

MARTY, F. L. *Teaching French* Audio-Visual Publications, Roanoke, Virginia, 1968

MATHIEU, G., ed. *Advances in the teaching of modern languages, vol. 2*, Pergamon 1966

PALMER, H. E. *The scientific study and teaching of languages* Harrap 1917; reprinted by Oxford University Press 1968

PALMER, H. E. *The principles of language-study* Harrap 1921; reprinted by Oxford University Press 1964

PALMER, H. E. *The oral method of teaching languages* Heffer, Cambridge, 1921; reprinted 1965

POLITZER, R. *Teaching French: an introduction to applied linguistics* Blaisdell, Waltham, Massachusetts: 2nd edn, 1965

RIVERS, W. M. *The psychologist and the foreign-language teacher* University of Chicago Press 1964

RIVERS, W. M. *Teaching foreign-language skills* University of Chicago Press 1968

RUSSELL, C. V., ed. *Post 'O' Level studies in modern languages* Pergamon 1970

SWEET, H. *The practical study of languages* Dent 1899; reprinted by Oxford University Press 1964

THIMANN, I. C. *Teaching languages* Harrap 1955

VALDMAN, A., ed. *Trends in language teaching* McGraw-Hill 1966

VERNON, P. J., ed. *The audio-visual approach to modern language teaching: a symposium* National Committee for Audio-Visual Aids in Education, London, 1965. New symposium 1973

2. *Audio-visual Aids*

CABLE, R. *Audio-visual handbook* University of London Press
1965

CORDER, S. P. *English language teaching and television* Longman
1960

ERICKSON, C. W. H. *Fundamentals of teaching with audio-visual
technology* Collier-Macmillan 1965

HICKEL, R. *Modern language teaching by television* Council for
Cultural Co-operation of the Council of Europe, Strasbourg,
1965

JUDD, R. S. *Teaching by projection* The Focal Press, London and
New York, 1963

LEE, W. R. and COPPEN, H. *Simple audio-visual aids to foreign-
language teaching* Oxford University Press, 2nd edn, 1968

MIALARET, G. *The psychology of the use of audio-visual aids in
primary school education* UNESCO Publication Harrap 1966

NATIONAL COMMITTEE FOR AUDIO-VISUAL AIDS IN EDUCATION, 33
Queen Anne Street, London W1M 0AL, issue the following
publications:

Classroom display material (A. Vincent)

Wall sheets: their design, production and use (H. Coppen)

The overhead projector (A. Vincent)

8mm in education (H. C. Butler)

16mm sound film projectors (N.C.A.V.A.E.)

Film projecting without tears or technicalities (M. Simpson)

Lights please! (R. Leggat)

3. *Tape-Recorders*

BORWICK, J. *The Emitape guide to better recording* E.M.I. Tape
Ltd. Hayes, Middlesex, 3rd edn, 1965

JONES, J. G. *Teaching with tape* The Focal Press, London and
New York, 1962

PURVES, F. *The Grundig book* The Focal Press, London and New
York, 12th edn, 1968

WESTON, J. *The tape recorder in the classroom* National Committee for Audio-Visual Aids in Education, 3rd edn, 1968

WOOD, D. N. *On tape: the creative use of the tape recorder* Ward Lock Educational 1969

4. Language Laboratories

ADAM, J. B. and SHAWCROSS, A. J. *The language laboratory* Pitman 1963

DEPARTMENT OF EDUCATION AND SCIENCE *Language laboratories* Education survey no. 3, HMSO, 1968

DICKINSON, L., DAKIN, L., HOWATT, A. P. R., LOCKE, P. *The language laboratory* Longman 1973

HAYES, A. S. *Language laboratory facilities: technical guide for their selection, purchase, use and maintenance* Oxford University Press, 2nd edn, 1968

HILTON, J. B. *The language laboratory in school* Methuen 1964

MARTY, F. L. *Language laboratory learning* Audio-Visual Publications, Wellesley, Massachusetts, 1960

MORTON, F. R. *The language laboratory as a teaching machine* University of Michigan 1961

SCOTTISH EDUCATION DEPARTMENT *The language laboratory in secondary schools* 1971

STACK, E. M. *The language laboratory and modern language teaching* Oxford University Press, 3rd edn, 1971

TURNER, J. D. *Introduction to the language laboratory* University of London Press 1965

TURNER, J. D., ed. *Programming for the language laboratory* University of London Press 1968

TURNER, J. D., ed. *Using the language laboratory* University of London Press 1969

VERNON, P. J., ed. *The use of language laboratories in Great Britain* National Committee for Audio-Visual Aids in Education 1965

Chapter Notes

Chapter 1

The reader who is interested in analysing classroom performance by studying what the teacher does and what the pupils do, is referred to NELSON, L. N., ed. *The nature of teaching: a collection of readings*, Blaisdell, 1969. The first section of this American publication (pp. 1–83) contains a number of short articles by various authors: *Teacher influence in the classroom; Teacher leadership: an empirical approach to analysing teacher behaviour in the classroom; Intent, action, and feedback: a preparation for teaching; Interaction analysis as a feedback system in teacher preparation.* Each article has a bibliography of selected books and articles. The 'framework of analysis' which appears at the end of the present book can be viewed against the background of such articles.

A basic work exemplifying the principles and practice of audio-lingual method is BROOKS. A critical review of the method is RIVERS (1964). Studies of teaching the listening and speaking skills can be found in Chapters 6, 7 and 8 of RIVERS (1968), Chapters 9 and 14 of MACKEY, and Chapters 6–9 of MARTY (1968).

A list of useful classroom expressions is found at the beginning of the Schools Council French course 'En avant' published by E. J. Arnold & Sons Ltd., Leeds, England.

To gain an understanding of the needs of the learner to respond to the material presented the reader is referred to such general texts as PEEL, E. A. *The psychological basis of education*, Oliver & Boyd, 2nd edn., 1967 (Chapters 1–6) and texts on programmed learning such as HOWATT, A. *Programmed learning and the language teacher*, Longman, 1969.

For a detailed analysis of how to frame and sequence questions see PALMER (1965). As an introduction to question work see Chapters 4 and 5 of COLE.

Chapter 2

The theory and practice of an audio-visual approach to language teaching is well exemplified in DUTTON (in the first section by J. JERMAN, pp. 1–83), HUEBENER (1967), VERNON, and Chapter 5 of HARDING.

Chapter 2 of COLE gives a brief introduction to using visual aids, pp. 18–32. LEE and COPPEN gives a fuller treatment. CORDER (1966) is a good study of the visual element in language teaching. CABLE and the various publications of the NATIONAL COMMITTEE FOR AUDIO-VISUAL AIDS IN EDUCATION are most useful in learning how to operate equipment. See also Sussex Survey detailed in notes to Chapter 10.

An introduction to using the tape-recorder is WESTON and to using the language laboratory TURNER (1965) and STACK (1971 edn). The publication of the DEPARTMENT OF EDUCATION AND SCIENCE is very practical and deals succintly with labs and how to use them. Chapter 6 of HARDING is good preliminary reading. Chapter 15 of MACKEY can provide a good starting-point, and Chapters 10 and 11 of MARTY make many useful observations on the operation of equipment in relation to the teaching situation.

Filmstrips form a central component of most 'audio-visual courses': see the annotated bibliographies of French, Spanish, German, Russian and Italian *Recorded and audio-visual materials*, published by the Centre for Information on Language Teaching and Research, State House, 63 High Holborn, London WC1R 4TN. In the French list one might quote 'Voix et images de France', 'TAVOR Aids audio-visual French course', 'Longman Audio-Visual French', 'Harrap-Didier audio-visual French' and 'Le français d'aujourd'hui'. See *Primary School French* for courses intended for young beginners, in particular 'Bonjour Line' and 'French through action'. Filmstrips can also be used in conjunction with readers: a very good series is 'Let's read

French' by P. Symonds, published by Oxford University Press. Filmstrips may also be used in a supplementary capacity to convey information on France and its 'civilisation' aspects: see the catalogues of the Educational Foundation for Visual Aids, 33 Queen Anne Street, London W1M 0AL, on 'Visual Aids' and 'Materials for Modern Languages'.

Harrap and European Schoolbooks both issue very good sets of slides on various aspects of France, French culture, and scenes for teaching material. A good example of slides used to teach grammatical points is G. Fleming's 'French visual grammar', Macmillan, 1968.

Good examples of cineloops are the set by G. Fleming, 'Les aventures de la famille Carré', Macmillan, and the French, Russian and German cineloops published by Longman.

The Institut français du Royaume-Uni, Queensberry Place, London S.W.7, list a whole range of 16mm films in their catalogue. As good examples of language teaching films the reader is referred to 'Toute la bande' and 'Portrait d'un village—Entrechaux' by Mary Glasgow Publications Ltd., Brookhampton Lane, Kineton, Warwicks., England. Also 'Dax' and 'Fête à Coutances'.

A set of useful transparencies for use on the overhead projector is that by A. Topping, 'Overhead French' published by G.A.F. (Great Britain) Ltd., Educational Programmes, Stourton House, Dacre Street, London S.W.1.

A good set of wallpictures, depicting twenty general scenes, is 'Que voyez-vous?' published by European Schoolbooks Ltd., 122 Bath Road, Cheltenham, Gloucestershire GL53 7JX, England. The same firm also publish domino, lotto and card games for group and class use. The French Packs by Longman contain workcards and topic cards. Figurines and flashcards are obtainable from E. J. Arnold and Son Ltd., Butterley Street, Leeds 10, Yorkshire, England.

Chapter 3

Much useful information on the general principles of preparing and presenting one's lessons is to be found in more basic texts such as HUGHES, A. G. and HUGHES, E. H. *Learning and teaching: an introduction to psychology and education*, Longmans, Green and Co. Ltd, 3rd edn. 1959: see for example Chapter 18 on 'The art of teaching', pp. 354–389, at the end of which a short list of other useful books is to be found. Another standard text from which young teachers can gather many practical 'tips' is WARD, H. and ROSCOE, F. *The approach to teaching*, Bell, 2nd edn. 1958: see for example Chapters 6 and 7. MILLS, H. R. *Teaching and training: techniques for instructors*, Macmillan, 1967, although intended for the occupational training of adults, gives much practical advice on general method. See for example Chapters 2–5.

To acquaint himself with the 'phases' of an audio-visual approach to language teaching the reader should read the introductory notes to each of the stages of the Schools Council French course 'En avant', mentioned in the notes to Chapter 1. More particularly he can refer to handbooks accompanying the 'Bonjour Line' course issued by Harrap and the 'Voix et images' course. LONG, J. G. *Teaching with 'Le français par la méthode audio-visuelle'*, Philadelphia and New York: Chilton Books, 1964, gives a readable and concise account of the same 'phases' as are used with the CREDIF 'Voix et images' issued by Harrap. The 'Teacher's Book' for 'Longman Audio-Visual French' contains at the beginning notes on the use of the course; the suggestions for presentation and for development are also valuable for distinguishing the various 'phases' of the teaching and learning process.

For exploitation work involving games see LEE, W. R. *Language-teaching games and contests*, Oxford University Press, 1965, and BUCKBY, M. *Faites vos jeux*, Materials Development Unit, Language Teaching Centre, University of York, England, 1971. The latter contains 165 games which practise specific linguistic points. For magazines in various languages see the advertising folders of Mary Glasgow Publications Ltd, Brookhampton Lane, Kineton, Warwicks., England. Three interesting French magazines for different levels: 'Feu vert', 'Quoi de neuf?' and 'Passe-partout', are published by Librairie Française Hachette, 4 Regent Place, London W1 R6 BH.

Chapter 4

The basic principle of learning a foreign language through actions and objects is extensively developed in GOUIN. Those books on method which give some emphasis to activity are BILLOWS, GURREY, FINOCCHIARO. See also Chapter 6 of COLE where specific examples of miming linked with sentence building are given. PALMER, H. E. and PALMER, D. *English through actions*, Longman, shows how a programme can stress the activity aspect with regard to beginners.

Many forms of activity work occur in the first stage of the Schools Council 'En avant' course. ROWLANDS, D., ed. *Group-work in modern languages*, Materials Development Unit, Language Teaching Centre, University of York, England, provides many suggestions for the operation of activity within group-work.

A fair range of dialogues and playlets exist from various publishers. The reader is referred to the Harrap Educational Reference List where the plays are grouped under elementary, intermediate, and advanced categories. For an example of a set of classroom playlets see ARNOLD, M. *En scène*, Hulton Educational Publications, 1971.

Chapter 5

Basic studies of learning and remembering in relation to school learning are found in most texts on educational psychology. The reader is referred to Chapter 9 of LOVELL, K. *Educational psychology and children*, University of London Press, and to Chapter 2 of PEEL, E. A. *The psychological basis of education*, Oliver & Boyd, 2nd edn. 1967.

The analysis of repetition in language teaching forms Chapter 9 of MACKEY. A critique of audio-lingual techniques that stress habit formation can be read in RIVERS (1964).

The advantages of using language laboratory facilities of various types are clearly argued in STACK. A realistic appraisal of using the laboratory in school is HILTON and, for a critical discussion, MARTY (1968) is thought-provoking. The two books edited by TURNER provide good coverage of the types of work done and materials used in language laboratories.

Classroom questioning procedures and matters of practical detail helpful to the beginning teacher are dealt with in DODSON. Many points of this chapter can be related closely to the question-and-answer techniques exemplified in PALMER (1965) and the principle of repetition expounded in the other two works by him quoted in the bibliography.

Chapter 6

Personality traits which make for a successful language teacher are briefly discussed in RIVERS (1964): see for example page 162. Chapters 2 and 5 of WARD, H. and ROSCOE, F. *The approach to teaching*, Bell, 2nd edn. 1958 provide the young teacher with a good deal of very useful advice on class discipline and relationships with pupils. VERITY, T. E. A. *On becoming a teacher*, University of London Press, 1954, is a useful introduction to many aspects of life as a teacher and contains many helpful observations on personality development. JOHNSON, E. *Teaching: a basic guide*, Harrap, 1969, also provides useful reading on coping with classes for the first time.

The treatment of questioning as a general teaching technique is developed in AUSTIN, F. M. *The art of questioning in the classroom*, University of London Press, 1949. DODSON gives guidance on practical procedures of question-and-answer work in the classroom. Chapters 4 and 5 of COLE are a good introduction to the subject; for a more extensive study see PALMER (1968) and for a systematic analysis of grouping and grading questions PALMER (1965).

Chapter 7

Chapter 1 of COLE argues the importance of listening comprehension as a preparation for developing oral proficiency. Discussions of listening comprehension occur in MACKEY: pp. 261–263 and some drills are given in Appendix A, and in Chapter 6 of RIVERS (1968). Chapter 5 of RIVERS (1964) deals with psychological aspects of hearing a foreign language. MARTY (1968) contains a thorough study of French phonology and makes a number of useful observations concerning comprehension of the spoken language.

For extensive illustration of what is meant by 'augmented questions' see PALMER (1965).

Technical specifications of tape-recorders and a discussion of standards of sound reproduction occur in WESTON. For the tehnicalities of the language laboratory HAYES is a very good study; this work also contains a good bibliography of articles relating to modern methodology. The Appendix to the DEPART-MENT OF EDUCATION AND SCIENCE Survey No. 3 is a concise summary of desirable and essential laboratory facilities. PURVES covers tapes, microphones, extension speakers, and so on besides the tape-recorder itself.

Preparedness and 'set' are concepts best appreciated within the context of RIVERS (1964); page 83 defines its significance. Pp. 345–346 of MACKEY also stress its importance in relation to the first minutes of a given lesson.

Chapter 8

An excellent account of ways in which structural drills can be contextualised is the article by B. Woolrich 'English as a foreign language' in TURNER (1968), pp. 27–92. Although examples are in English the basic principles apply in many cases to other foreign languages. Two good books dealing with structure drills and giving abundant examples of numerous types are RÉQUÉDAT, F. *Les exercices structuraux* (Collection Le français dans le monde, B.E.L.C.), Librairies Hachette et Larousse, 1966, and ETMEKJIAN, J. *Pattern drills in language teaching*, New York University Press and University of London Press, 1966.

BEAL, M. *French language drills*, Macmillan, 1967, in its later pages gives some drills to which principles of contextualisation have been applied. UPTON, L. K. *Talk French*, Mary Glasgow Publications Ltd, 1969, is a good example of material which employs visuals in conjunction with drills. Stages 4A, 4B and 5 of the Schools Council French course 'En avant', and Stages A3,

A4, A5, B3 and B4 of the Longman Audio-Visual French course contain many examples of linguistic points being contextualised and used in connection with visuals.

BUCKBY, M. *Faites vos jeux*, Materials Development Unit, Language Teaching Centre, University of York, England, 1971, provides much material which could be used to extend the procedures suggested in this chapter, European Schoolbooks Ltd., 122 Bath Road, Cheltenham, Gloucestershire, England, have a number of board and card games which could be utilised in group work in class. The Schools Council Foreign Languages Materials Development Unit are also producing small materials for use by groups and individuals within the class. The Longmans French Packs detailed in the Notes to Chapter 9 are also useful in this respect. ROWLANDS, D., ed. *Group-work in modern languages*, Materials Development Unit, Language Teaching Centre, University of York, is another helpful Schools Council publication. It refers in its first part to the Primary School and in its second part to the Secondary School and provides fruitful lines of approach.

Chapter 9

The Longman French Packs have 'civilisation' as the central component: 'La vie en France', 'pays de France', 'Histoire de France', 1972. Harrap produces sets of slides which focus attention on aspects of life in France, 'Vie quotidienne' and of the geography of France, 'À la découverte de la France'. The 'Éditions Bordas' of Harrap contain not only texts of a literary nature but also texts on history, geography (including political and economics atlases), zoology, botany, physics, chemistry, biological sciences, philosophy, mathematics, psychology and other topics such as railways and telecommunications. For books in French on these subjects see the most recent of Harrap's Educational Reference List. Hachette, also, publishes a number of history and geography texts, besides the illustrated review 'Documentation pédagogique' and the excellent 'Guide France' by G. Michaud.

An exhibition of textbooks in French is lent out to Local

Education Authorities by the French Embassy in London. An extensive annotated bibliography of books and audio-visual materials on 'civilisation' aspects can be found in the *European studies handbook* prepared by P. Freeman and issued by the Centre for Contemporary European Studies, University of Sussex, 1970, with its Supplements. From the same source comes a useful survey *Patterns of teaching about contemporary Europe in secondary schools*, by M. Wheatcroft and P. Freeman, January 1972.

Many of the materials listed in the bibliographies produced by the Centre for Information on Language Teaching and Research, State House, 63 High Holborn, London WC1R 4TN, contain 'civilisation' elements. One might examine, for example, the French, German, Spanish, Russian and Italian *Recorded and audio-visual materials*. Many 'readers' also focus on the 'civilisation' aspects: COURTNEY, G. *Je vous présente*, Longman, 1966; LEESON, R. *Voyage à Paris*, Longman, 1967; the series by ROE, C. entitled 'Les jeunes travaillent', Longman, 1971.

A good example of a Sixth Form course stressing 'civilisation' is NOTT, D. O. and TRICKEY, J. E. *Actualités françaises*, English Universities Press, 1970, which includes tapes.

Slides, games and aids which stress aspects of France and French life are obtainable from European Schoolbooks Ltd., 122 Bath Road, Cheltenham, Gloucestershire, England. Film catalogues worth studying are those of the Educational Foundation for Visual Aids, 33 Queen Anne Street, London W1M 0AL, and of the Institut français du Royaume-Uni, Service du cinéma, Queensberry Place, London S.W.7.

The reader wishing to consult more detailed and extensive bibliographical information on all aspects of the audio-visual presentation of the 'civilisation' of France is referred to services of the Institut pédagogique national, 29 rue d'Ulm, Paris-5ᵉ, and of the Bureau pour l'enseignement de la langue et de la civilisation française à l'étranger (B.E.L.C.), 9 rue Lhomond, Paris-5ᵉ. The journal 'Le français dans le monde' appears eight times a year and contains often useful references to material which can be exploited for 'civilisation' teaching. It can be obtained through Hachette, 4 Regent Place, London W1 R6BH. Hachette also publish a periodical review 'Books from France'. An excellent series for the advanced student, obtainable from the same source, is 'Que sais-je?' which includes over 1,500 titles on different subjects and topics.

Chapter 10

A good comprehensive text which covers some of the matters raised in this chapter and places language teaching within a general context of curriculum development is that of the Incorporated Association of Assistant Masters in Secondary Schools, *The teaching of modern languages*, University of London Press, 4th edn. 1967. The reader is also referred for an overall view to the Schools Council Working Paper No. 19, *Development of modern language teaching in secondary schools*, HMSO, 1969.

For a view of Sixth Form objectives see Schools Council Working Paper No. 28, *New patterns in sixth form modern language studies*, London: Evans Brothers Ltd. and Methuen Educational Ltd., 1970.

For an informative survey of the problems of using audio-visual equipment in schools see the publication *Audio-visual resources in Sussex schools* by MACKENZIE N., JONES H. C. and PAYNE T., Centre for Educational Technology at the University of Sussex.

The Reports and Papers published by the Centre for Information on Language Teaching and Research, State House, 63 High Holborn, London WC1R 4TN, are helpful in gaining a broad view of aims and purposes in language teaching. In particular the reader is referred to *Aims and techniques*, Paper No. 2, September 1969, and *Teaching modern languages across the ability range*, Paper No. 8, September 1972.

The principles of gradation and proportion are fully expounded in PALMER (1964). Chapter 7 of MACKEY deals with gradation and Chapter 10 deals with the measurement of method, including gradation. Proportion is examined on pp. 358–360 of MACKEY, and the lesson plan is analysed in Chapter 13.

Index